"Can a distinction be made between poetic language and the privileged language of the philosopher?" (p. 52)

"Transcendence, in contemporary poetry, may disrupt and bewilder apophansis, which is unable to embrace its epos in terms... that do not rejoin their identity" (p. 87)

Celan suggests that "poetry may be an unheard modality of the <u>otherwise than being</u>" (p. 46)

MERIDIAN

Crossing Aesthetics

Werner Hamacher
& David E. Wellbery
Editors

Translated by
Michael B. Smith

Stanford
University
Press

Stanford
California
1996

PROPER NAMES

Emmanuel Levinas

Stanford University Press
Stanford, California
© 1975, 1976 Editions Fata Morgana,
    Noms propres and *Sur Maurice Blanchot*
English translation and Introduction,
    Foreword, Notes and Bibliography
    © 1996 The Athlone Press
Originating publisher of English edition:
    The Athlone Press, London
First published in the U.S.A. by
    Stanford University Press, 1996
Printed in Great Britain
Cloth ISBN 0–8047–2351–6
Paper   ISBN 0–8047–2352–4
LC 93–86851
This book is printed on acid-free paper.

Contents

Acknowledgments ix

Bibliographical Information xi

Proper Names

Foreword 3

1 Poetry and Resurrection: Notes on Agnon 7

2 Martin Buber and the Theory of Knowledge 17

3 Dialogue with Martin Buber 36

4 Paul Celan: From Being to the Other 40

5 Jeanne Delhomme: Penelope, or Modal Thought 47

6 Jacques Derrida: Wholly Otherwise 55

7 Edmond Jabès Today 63

8 Kierkegaard: Existence and Ethics 66

9 A Propos of "Kierkegaard vivant" 75

10 Jean Lacroix: Philosophy and Religion 80

11 Roger Laporte and the Still Small Voice 90

12 Max Picard and the Face 94

13 The Other in Proust 99

14 Father Herman Leo Van Breda 106

15 Jean Wahl and Feeling 110

16 Nameless 119

On Maurice Blanchot

1 The Poet's Vision 127
2 The Servant and Her Master 140
3 A Conversation with André Dalmas 150
4 Exercises on "The Madness of the Day" 156

Notes 171
Index 189

Acknowledgments

The translator wishes to thank Berry College in general, and in particular Kathy Gann, Assistant Director of Faculty Research and Sponsored Programs, Lance Foldes, Director of the College Library, and his student assistant, Sheryl Bielewski, for their help in bringing this translation project to fruition. A special thanks to Jenny Overton for judicious text editing, to Jill Robbins for her knowledgeable suggestions, to Catherine Chalier for her help with several interpretations of, and annotations to, the text, and especially to his wife Helen for her sustaining encouragement.

To Simone, Georgie and Michael
To David, Valérie, Juliette and Boris

Bibliographical Information

Proper Names

"Poetry and Resurrection: Notes on Agnon" appeared in *Les Nouveaux Cahiers* (32 [1973]).

"Martin Buber and the Theory of Knowledge" was published in *Philosophie des 20. Jahrhunderts* (Stuttgart: Kohlhammer, 1963), and written in 1958.

"Dialogue with Martin Buber" appeared in *Les Nouveaux Cahiers* (3 [1965]).

"Paul Celan: From Being to the Other" appeared in *Revue des Belles-Lettres* (2–3 [1972]).

"Jeanne Delhomme: Penelope, or Modal Thought" was published in *Critique* (237 [1967]).

"Jacques Derrida: Wholly Otherwise" was published in *L'Arc* (54 [1973]).

"Edmond Jabès Today" appeared in *Les Nouveaux Cahiers* (31 [1972–1973]).

"Kierkegaard: Existence and Ethics" was published (in German) in *Schweizer Monatshefte* (43 [1963]).

"A Propos of 'Kierkegaard vivant'" consists of two interventions by Levinas originally published in *Kierkegaard vivant* (Paris: Gallimard, Collection "Idées" no. 106, 1966), modified and preceded by an introductory note for publication in *Noms propres.*

"Jean Lacroix: Philosophy and Religion" was published in *Critique* (289 [1971]).

"Roger Laporte and the Still Small Voice" appeared in *La Nouvelle Revue Française* (168 [1966]).

"Max Picard and the Face" is the first publication of a paper read on March 22, 1966 at a meeting of the Jeunesse Littéraire de France to honor the memory of Max Picard.

"The Other in Proust" was published in *Deucalion* (2 [1947]).

"Father Herman Leo Van Breda" was published in *Bulletin de la Société française de Philosophie* (67 [1973]).

"Jean Wahl and Feeling" appeared in *Cahiers du Sud* (331 [1955]).

"Nameless" was published under the title "Honneur sans Drapeau" [Honor without Flag] in *Les Nouveaux Cahiers* (6 [1966]).

On Maurice Blanchot

"The Poet's Vision" appeared in *Monde Nouveau* (98 [1956]).

"The Servant and Her Master" was published in *Critique* (229 [1966]).

"A Conversation with André Dalmas" was published in *La Quinzaine Littéraire* (115 [1971]).

"Exercises on 'The Madness of the Day'" appeared in *Change* (22 [1975]).

PROPER NAMES

Foreword

The world wars (and local ones), National Socialism, Stalinism (and even de-Stalinization), the camps, the gas chambers, nuclear weapons, terrorism and unemployment—that is a lot for just one generation, even for those who were but onlookers.

Yet we marveled, while still in school, at the prospects for renewal recently introduced by Bergson's conception of *durée*. We learned, with Husserl, how to be clear about what we thought by exploring *how* we thought it: thereby avoiding the slippage of meaning brought about by the mind's unrecognized intentionality, and discovering that Being dictates its ways of *appearing* in us. And thanks to Heidegger our ears learned to hear being in its verbal resonance—a reverberation never heard before, and henceforth unforgettable. That new sound would give us access to being itself, to the will that wills not to will, and to the generosity that lets Being be: *Gelassenheit*. Perhaps this last term should have been translated into French as *déception* in the etymological sense [release, from the Latin *decapio*], thereby suggesting that *déception* in its direct meaning [disappointment] may not be the only possible condition for *dis-inter-estedness*. But then some among us had other reasons to be disappointed.[1]

In any case, at no other time has historical experience weighed so heavily upon ideas; or, at least, never before have the members of one generation been more aware of that weight. In the twenty-five centuries during which our civilization has been chronicled, the Impregnable Rock of God, the *fundamentum inconcussum* of the *cogito*, and the Starry Heavens of the World, have, in that order, stemmed time's flow and secured a presence for the present. But now theories on the death of God, the contingency of humanness in philosophical reflection and the bankruptcy of humanism—doctrines already voiced by the end of the last century—have taken on apocalyptic proportions. The new anxiety, that of language cast adrift, seems to announce— without periphrases, which are henceforth impossible or deprived of all persuasive force—the end of the world.

Time no longer conveys its meaning in the simultaneity of sentences. Statements no longer succeed in putting things together. "Signifiers" without "signifieds" play a "sign game" with neither sense nor stakes. It is as if Plato's anamnesis, which for centuries maintained the unity of representation, were becoming amnesia—as if disorder did not necessarily re-establish a different order.[2] There is a general alienation from the meaningful as posited—from Husserl's "doxic thesis"; an opposition to the rigor of logical forms, adjudged to be repressive; an obsession with the inexpressible, the ineffable, the unsaid—which are sought in the awkward expression, the slip of the tongue, the scatological. Genealogy as exegesis, the dead bodies of words swollen with etymologies and devoid of *logos*, borne by the drift of the texts: such is modernity, in its painful break with discourse, as witnessed by its most sincere representatives. But a modernity that is already degenerating into elementary truths and fashionable banter.

Perhaps the names of persons whose *saying* signifies a face— proper names, in the middle of all these common names and commonplaces—can resist the dissolution of meaning and help us to speak. Perhaps they will enable us to divine, behind the downfall of discourse, the end of a certain *intelligibility* but the dawning of a new one. What is coming to a close may be a rationality tied *exclusively* to the being that is sustained by words, the *Said* of the Saying, the Said conveying fields of knowledge and truths in the form of unchanging identities, merging with the self-sufficient Identity of a being or system—complete, perfect, denying or absorbing the differences that appear to betray or limit it. This intelligibility reaches its apotheosis in the ultimate identity of "the identical and the non-identical" asserted by Hegel, which probably completes and concludes the philosophy of the Same and of immanence, or ontology.

Jean Wahl, in a collection published three years after the Second World War, called *Poésie, pensée, perception* [Poetry, Thought, Perception], noted (on page 253) under the word "absolute": "It is first of all the idea of that which is separated. It has become the idea of the complete, the encompassing. The non-encompassed has become the encompassing. Should we not return to the first meaning? Doesn't the second lead us to Hegel and the new Hegelians?" And Wahl tries to get back to that absolute, which is separate or transcendent, in the intensity of the felt, of passion, of poetry.

But already immediately after the First World War Gabriel Marcel, in his *Metaphysical Journal,* challenged "the classical idea, the eminent value of *autarkia,* or personal self-sufficiency."

> The perfect is not what is sufficient unto itself—or at any rate that perfection is the perfection of a system, not of a being. On what condition can the relationship between a being and what it needs represent a spiritual value? It seems there must be reciprocity, an awakening. Only a relationship of being to being can be called spiritual. ... What counts here is the spiritual exchange between beings; here it is not a question of respect but of love.[3]

This is an important text, even though there is a lot about being, spirit, the spiritual and love in it—words that, for today's tastes, may seem the verbal incontinence of a defunct idealism. True, they abound in Marcel's later works—but what matter? Here being is not consciousness of self; it is relation to the other than self, and awakening. And the other than self—is that not the Other [*Autrui*]? And love means, before all else, the welcoming of the other as *thou.* Can that welcome be carried out empty-handed? The full importance of my fellow human being's need for *food* and *drink*—all philanthropic mystification aside—bursts forth from the serenity of the categories and commands them. This is a form of intelligibility that goes from the Same to the Other without suppressing difference. Spirit is no longer the *Said* once and for all. It is the *Saying* that always opens up a passage from the Same to the Other, where there is as yet nothing in common. A non-indifference of one toward the other! Beneath the spirituality of the *I,* awakened by the *thou* in Marcel's work, converging with Buber and an entire philosophy that believes itself to be a philosophy of dialogue, a (that is also very old) new signifying signifies: that of the Gift and sacrifice. What I call the non-in-difference of Saying is, below the double negation, still difference, behind which no commonality arises in the form of an entity. Thus there is both relation and rupture, and thus awakening: awakening of the Self by the Other, of me by the Stranger, of me by the stateless person, that is, by the neighbor who is only nearby. An awakening that is neither reflection upon oneself nor universalization. An awakening signifying a responsibility for the other, the other who must be fed and clothed—my substitution for the other, my expiation for the suffering, and no doubt for the wrongdoing of the other. An expiation assigned to me without any possible avoidance, and by which my uniqueness as myself, instead of being alienated, is intensified by my irreplaceability.

But in that rupture and that awakening and that expiation and that intensification the divine comedy of a transcendence beyond ontology unfolds.

1 Poetry and Resurrection: Notes on Agnon

In memory of Muriel Lévy
and Henri Dombrowner

I

Does Agnon belong to the world of the Jewish tradition to which the best-known and most admired part of his work is devoted? Or does he, on the contrary, bear witness to the breakdown, the collapse, the end of that world, and consequently (to use an already popular phrase) is he "seized by the anguish of the modern world?" This dilemma can be justified only to the extent that a poetic work is at the same time a document, and the art that went into its making is at once a use of discourse. This discourse deals with objects that are also spoken of in the newspapers, posters, memoirs and letters of every passing age—though in the case of poetry's strictly poetic expression these objects merely furnish a favorable occasion and serve as pretexts. It is of the essence of art to signify only between the lines—in the intervals of time, between times—like a footprint that would precede the step, or an echo preceding the sound of a voice. Only exegesis, after the fact, completes and repeats again, indefinitely, that step and that call. Such is the anachronism that is probably one of the modalities of inspiration. In this there is no belittling of the literal meaning. The letters bordering the inter-linear trace remain, in literature, a refined, suggestive language, through imagery and metaphors, from which no speaking is exempt. Teachers must bring this aspect out for their students: those who would learn to read must be able to distinguish the literal from the poetic meaning.

And Agnon's language, and the life it lets speak (whether in its wholeness or its disintegration), and the land of Israel it conjures up—all that is intertwined with books, it issues from books or returns to them. It all goes back to a past concerning which we are justified in wondering whether it could ever have been contained within a present, and whether today it can be re-presented. Poetry *signifies* it, but not in its theme. It signifies it as song. Its song cannot be reduced to the perfect harmony between the Saying and the Said attributable to the writer's *craft*, nor to the "author's love for his people, religion or language" (to the *ahavat Israel*),[1] which, being a real feeling, would explain his literary work as *work*. All craft, allegiance or commitment aside, the quest for a certain sound (and a sense unsayable without it) finds in Agnon—in that language, that life, that land—a full-range instrument for its expression.

Here is a living, modern language, but one whose birth was a resurrection, a raising up from the depths of the Scriptures, a life emerging from the frozen swirl of letters fixing oral discussion and traditions. Beneath the froth, like an intricate lace, stands the minute script of commentaries on commentaries. The dead language of the Scriptures, in which each expression stands in its final, inviolable space. But is it a death—immobility pure and simple? Or is it the way for a Saying to *seek* the ineffable, beyond the place where memory gives itself memories? Writing as inter-rogation. Interrogation as relationship. What an evolution at the heart of that eternity of the question lodged in the books! From generation to generation, daring, eager eyes have scrutinized them, sounding them, turning them this way and that,[2] in order to enter into the static movement of the signs that go toward the "deep past" of these superimposed texts, though never reaching it.

A living, a resuscitated language, whose words are summoned to signify, among the living, things of the present and things hoped for. But is that a life, beneath the persistent dream that these words convey, beneath the ineradicable memory of their semantic homeland in the texts? There is an ambiguity or an enigma about the Hebrew word. Long before Agnon, this was one of the resources of the *melitsah*:[3] the sentence would use biblical turns of phrase, achieving a rhetorical effect thereby, with no quotation marks needed for the experienced reader. This trope in Agnon's writing becomes the breaking-away from a certain ontology. A reference to biblical or rabbinic writings, the repetition of the master formulation, a variant or an echo—and suddenly the word, without imitating any model, signifies both in the context of the passage in which it occurs and, in counterpoint, in the scriptural context, oriented toward an unrepresentable past. Such is the enigmatic modality of a resuscitated language, beginning again within its own trace! The Jewish way of life signified in this ambiguous form of speech belongs to its mode of expression not only in the way a theme belongs to discourse. By its "mode of existence" that way of life prolongs and redoubles the enigma. The community of Israel and the things pertaining to its exile, and the land regained—these do not have any beginning in the being they spell out! They attest to that past through ritual that pervades the material gestures of existence, which have been diverted from their natural ends toward the symbol. It is as if the land meant nothing but the promise of land, as if the body and its organs had been created to carry out the commandments, as if fruit ripened on the trees only to occasion benedictions, and food were consumed for giving thanks—as if the seriousness of death were only in the fear (so it was seen one day by one of the greats in Israel) of seeing the pretext for so many liturgical movements disappear. It is a life that, properly speaking, does not make up a world. How can we express that modality, which is totally different from being? Would not the word *beyond* be adequate here? Not at all because of religion, which teaches of the *beyond*. The opposite would be closer to the truth: it is because the nature of things and beings has issued forth from the symbol, and because the delimiting of their rigorous essence is less true than their symbolism, that religion becomes plausible. Religion (or, more precisely, Judaism) would be the way in which a de-substantiation of being is of itself procured, of itself possible—an excluded middle in which the limits between life and non-life disappear. This modality is diametrically opposed to the reality of the substrata, sculpture-being, architecture and structure-being, solid being, each term of which begins in its own causality, and, nucleate, sustains itself. The symbolism of the rite, like the enigma of the Hebraic mode of expression [*dire*], de-nucleates ultimate solidity beneath the plasticity of forms, as taught by Western ontology.[4]

This modality is also completely different from the one that typifies another great poet of the surreal, Gogol, in whose works the Uncanny is incapable of shaking the solidity of the substratum. The extraordinary event of the Nose that posits itself *in itself*, in opposition to its own face (the petrified, self-satisfied face of Major Kovaleff), and rides in a coach dressed as a general, does not upset the normal course of events. Without causing a scandal, this nose gets involved in the blunderings of the police, personal correspondence, a doctor's professional habits, and the daily practice of a newspaper's want ads.

The Jewish way of life, rechanneled by the rite from its beginning and development in nature, thus mirrors, in Agnon, the sonority of the language in which it is expressed; the ambiguity of the present-day words resounds in the text from out of their dream. That life is not just sung; it is itself song. That is probably what lies at the root of the strictly untranslatable dimension of Agnon's work. Hence we may read Agnon as pure poetry, without bothering to try to determine whether the traditionalism he "describes" is, to him, unshakeable certainty, or a refuge, or the end of the world. The poetic meaning of the work transcends the anecdotal or social curiosities, the narrative or fictive element in which it is sought.

The bygone life of the diaspora, the land of Israel (its geography absorbed by history, that land palpitating within the words that designate it, emerging, like the words themselves, from the depths of books), offers Agnon's language a necessary prolongation. If they did not exist it would be necessary to invent them. Is it absolutely certain that Agnon didn't invent them, so that the symbols would symbolize symbols, so that a symbolism of symbolism would be possible—this language of language, the Song of songs, the resonance of one language on several registers, receiving from this formalism a proper meaning? There is a poetic meaning of the work that would not be convincing without the work, and that ceases so to be the moment it is presented as the simple said of this Saying.

That *beyond* is perhaps never more meaningful than when Agnon limits himself to reshuffling the elements of that reality (be it made up or not), letting us hear the rustle of that surreality: the enumeration of objects, the listing of proper names and names of rabbinical doctors, the tracing out of an itinerary in Israel, as followed by a person or even a dog, complete with the names of quarters, streets, houses, the description of a series of familiar or ritual gestures.

When we ate or drank I was honored by being asked to say the Seven Blessings. Two cups were filled; I took one in my hand and said in a high, soft voice: *keep away pain and anger.* And I blessed Him in whose house joy resides. And when I came to the passage that begins with *Have mercy,* I said, as is my custom: *"and may we not stumble."* I felt the bride looking at me even though I kept my eyes closed, after the custom of those who say that blessing. I felt her looking at me and closed my eyes tighter, so my thoughts would not be severed from Him who was being blessed. After the benediction, I put down the first cup and took the second, and said the blessings that end with *He who has created everything for his Glory,* and *He who created the human being,* and *He who gladdens Zion by his children,* and *He who gladdens the groom and the bride,* and *He who gladdens the groom with the bride.* And I lifted the first cup again and said the blessing for wine, and I drank from both cups, and I gave the bride and groom to drink, and all the guests, and I said the blessing *for the vine and the fruit of the vine*, and I disengaged myself and withdrew.[5]

The description takes up almost textually the commendations and the phrases of the rite. But in Agnon things reverberate, as if engendered by the ritual act, with all their "unrepresentability," as, in his language, the word's current meaning carries the clear but mysterious sonority of the Scripture. A marvel of the imagination? But the imagination is the presence of images. It represents substrata of being, once again destined for death, already cut off from the relation that, beyond Reminiscence, through the problematic of the Scripture, goes toward the unrepresentable past. In Agnon, what is at stake is resurrection. Closer to us than any present, the Unrepresentable will not be represented in the poem. It will be the poetry of the poem. Poetry *signifies* poetically the resurrection that sustains it: not in the fable it sings, but in its very singing.

II

The traditional Jewish "universe" in which being is meaning (and the reference to an Unrepresentable, and a continual fission, so to speak, of anything that might risk forming a nucleus of self-interest in that domain, as a substratum) provides Agnon with more than just a theme. It prolongs the *Saying* beneath the very modality of this Saying, in which the signifying of the Scripture resonates within the inmost reaches of the living word. There, between the present and that which has never been able to join a present, is situated the "between times" of poetry or resurrection.

But resurrection is the explicit concern of the last part of Agnon's last collection of texts, *Ha Esh Veha Etzim*—'The Fire and the Wood".[6] Is this a title or a question? The words refer indisputably to the fire and wood of the gas chambers, but they are taken from the question that Isaac, walking behind his father toward Moria mountain, asked Abraham: "Behold the fire and

the wood: but where is the lamb for a burnt offering?"[7]
Everything is a question in this text, and in the next to last story
in this collection, "The Sign." These are questions without
answers, to be taken note of in their very interrogativity. In "The
Sign," the author, settled in the land of the ancestors, learns, on
the eve of Shavuot, the news of the extermination by the
Germans of all the Jews in the Polish town where he was born.
It is impossible to summarize this tale, so rich in implications.
Life is in death, death in life. The festival commemorating the
giving of the Torah—the advent of meaning in being—is placed
at the heart of a mourning beyond words. And despair lies
hidden within the joy that remains the triumphant law of the
festival. The flowers and aromas of the regained land of Israel are
intermingled with the traces of blood and the taste of ashes; and
from the depths of their nothingness all the dead from his town
return in the poet's visions. He sees them again in their absolute
place. A place that is not a site, not a landscape into which
human beings blend; a place that is their place in the synagogues
of the vanished town, in which presence is elevation, in which
place is already non-place.

> And as for me, I found myself in the middle of my town as if the
> time of the resurrection of the dead had come. Great is the day of
> the resurrection of the dead! I had a bit of the taste of that day when
> I suddenly found myself among my fellow townsfolk, my dead
> brothers (who have "gone back to their world") before me, as they
> were during their lives in all the houses of prayer in my town.[8] …
> Standing there, feeling worried, I gazed at the inhabitants of my
> town and there was no hint of reproach in their eyes for the fact that
> *I was like this* and that *they were like that.*[9] But they were sad with a
> great and terrible sadness; except for one old man who had a kind of
> smile on his lips that seemed to be saying: the plunge had been
> taken. That is to say, we have taken the plunge and left the world of
> cares behind us.

There is equality between the dead and the living, except that
some are "like this" and the others are "like that"! In their places,

at their posts, beyond their own being, no longer speaking in the first person yet speaking to us—are the dead not freed from death, resuscitated in their very death? Only the living would ask for more existence—not understanding the meaning of the existence of Israel!

But in another vision, the poet sees again, in the town now deserted, two survivors, Haim the beadle and Shalom the cobbler.

> I said to them: "Let me ask you one more question. You said that after the second catastrophe no one was left alive in the town. So you are yourselves no longer alive!" They smiled, then, as the dead smile when they see that we think they are no longer alive.[10]

An enigmatic ontology, an enigmatic smile. An enigma set within the enigma. Does not this smile also express the irony the dead have toward themselves? Are the living completely wrong? Are eternity and resurrection through poetry free of all illusion? Are language and poetry the ultimate meaning of humanness?

There are grounds for surmising that perhaps the last pages of the text we are considering venture deliberately out beyond language. Here, in these pages, appears the poet Ibn Gabirol, whose poems, since the Middle Ages, have been a part of the liturgy for the festivals, and who doubtless inspired Agnon's own poetic vocation. The dead poet [Gabirol], in his compassion for him who weeps for the exterminated community of his native town, composes a poem on the vanished town that will be its sign. The name of the town appears as an acrostic in the poem. But the living poet [Agnon], in his very delight, forgets the poem as he listens to it. He is persuaded that this poem is chanted in the higher heavens by the saintly singers beloved of the Holy Name. But he laments: "Who will chant this poem to me?" In a world in which the living community is disappearing, who will be able to transmit the tradition itself? Who will be able to read the Scriptures? The mortality of the tradition reveals the rhetoric concealed by poetry—that last refuge of transcendence in

Western humanism. Agnon's anguish—that is its focal point. It
is not anguish over the end of traditional Jewish life, but over the
possible end of the literature that could bring it back to life,
before the crisis of Western humanism.

[handwritten marginalia: "anguish..." / "over the" / "possible end" / "of literature"]

III

Yet there is perhaps in "The Sign," in the form of a response
to that crisis (as if Agnon were also a respondent!), the indication
of an order, older than Saying, by which the non-sense of death
is put in question, by which the resurrection begins in death
itself—as the entire story continually suggests.

> Six million Jews assassinated by the Gentiles among us. A third of
> Israel has been killed, and the other two-thirds are orphaned. There is
> no one in Israel who does not have several dozen dead among his or
> her close relatives. The lights commemorating the disappeared burn as
> one sole light. Their brightness is the same. There is no difference
> between the light that has been lit to commemorate the soul of one
> who has exhausted the full measure of his days, and the soul of one
> who has been murdered. In heaven surely the one light is distinguished
> from the other, just as each soul is distinguished. It was a great thought
> that He who lives eternally had, to have chosen us from among all
> the peoples, to give us the Torah of Life, although it is a little diffi-
> cult to understand why he created, facing us, a kind of human
> beings that would take our lives because we observe the Torah.[11]

Why, as Agnon contemplates the lights commemorating the
departed, some in memory of victims of extermination, others in
memory of those who died a natural death, does he see in both
the same brightness—while hoping that "on high" they will be
distinguished from one another? Why else than because he
recognized the unity of Israel, that is, the inevitable binding into
a community of those human beings who are dedicated to the
other man? Why else than because he also saw that each one
within that community, whatever his or her destiny or death,
finds a personal meaning through belonging to the whole?

Why, at that moment, does Agnon bless the Eternal for having given Israel the Torah of Life, if not to recognize in the Law of justice and of love for one's neighbor (in the ethics humiliated by philosophers, and unknown to the violent) the signifyingness of all signification, stronger than death? That is, worthy of the supreme sacrifice, and thus signifying non-death in death?

Why is a reservation added to that blessing? Why, unresigned, is he surprised that murderers should deal death to those who keep the Torah of Life, if not to recognize Evil in evil and Death in death, if not to avoid comfortable theodicies, consolations that cost us nothing and compassion without suffering? If not to recognize also the mad meaning of the mystery of death? If everything were comprehensible in death, as a reasonable enterprise, it would fit into the limits of life. It would lose the surplus with which it exalts life. Life, sustaining its allegiances to the confines of death, thus goes beyond its being, its limits reaching beyond those limits; and, beyond being, it tastes the taste of the Resurrection.

2 Martin Buber and the Theory of Knowledge

1 The Question of Truth

The theory of knowledge is a theory of truth.[1] It asks, with Plato in the *Parmenides*: How can absolute being be manifested in truth? Does it not, by the fact of its manifestation, enter a world in which error is possible? If so, how then can an existence subject to error touch being without degrading it? Perhaps the entire effort of ancient philosophy was devoted to mediating the chasm separating the realms of appearance and being: a chasm that, within one universe, cannot possibly be unbridgeable. The soul need not leave itself to rejoin the One from which it has descended.

The question of the relationship between the subject and the object posed by the theory of knowledge in the modern period prolongs the classical question of truth. But it no longer presupposes the knowing subject, installed in its place within the hierarchy of beings that constitute the universe. The being who aspires to truth is radically separated from being. The idea of separation, thought through to the end, leads philosophers to seek, for separated being, a *sui generis* origin. The separated being is interpreted and posited on the basis of an interiority that is characterized specifically by not leading to anything *other*, in a dimension that leads only to itself. Separate existence becomes the knowing subject, or consciousness. Consciousness, in this scheme of things, is not just one of the soul's activities (even if it were to be the highest of them), but its substantiality as an isolated entity—that through which it exists on its own, i.e. separately; for to consciousness—the knowledge which accompanies every motion of the soul—nothing is external. Every motion of the soul—even one that puts it into relation with the outside world, such as affirmation, negation, volition, or one that expresses a dependence on the outer world, such as feeling—is, after all, a *thought* in the Cartesian sense. Consciousness, in which the existence of these motions is ultimately caught up (science being included in that consciousness), draws out from within itself all that comes from the outside. If the subject is posited as consciousness, whatever event occurs within it (whether consciousness be overwhelmed, jolted, or wounded) comes from this subject who becomes conscious, who thus exists on its own, and so is separate. Philosophy becomes, to use one of Husserl's terms, an egology. If Husserlian phenomenology, which has been such a powerful force in getting beyond the idealists' notion of the subject, remains an egology and recovers the universe in a constituting subject, it is because it never gave up interpreting the self as representative consciousness.

Hence the theory of knowledge, in the modern sense of the term, takes on a principiant value: it leads us to *original being*. The subject has this distinction precisely as the subject of knowledge. Thus the theory of knowledge precedes all other philosophical research, not only as a propaedeutic of knowledge, but as a theory of the absolute. Knowledge—the work, life and being of this being—is the relation to an object. But the object, which the subject constitutes as opposite, opposes the subject with an opposition that remains an even match for the thought it denies.

Common to both the ontology and the theory of the subject/object relation is an idea of truth as "sayable," and thus—whatever may be the structure of the being it reveals—as truth *qua* content. Truth is expressed by words, the original function of which is to signify a signification upon which solitary, silent thought may be sustained; not to speak to someone else. With that possibility of expressing, of saying truth, with the possibility of truth's being a result, all the monumental solidity of being returns; even if, since Plato's *Parmenides* and *The Sophist*, being is interpreted as relation, and, since Descartes, as thought; and even if the object becomes the intelligible but unrepresentable object of physical-mathematical science. One of the most interesting positions of the philosophy of Buber is to show that truth is not a content and that words do not contain it. It is more subjective than all subjectivity, but that extreme subjectivity, which is distinct from the subjectivity of the idealist subject, is the sole access to that which is more "objective" than all objectivity, to that which no subject ever contains, to the totally *other.*

But Buber's quest is connected with an entire movement in contemporary thought.

2 From Object to Being

The history of the theory of knowledge in contemporary philosophy is the history of the disappearance of the subject/object problem. Contemporary philosophy denounces as an abstraction the subject closed in upon itself and metaphysically the origin of itself and the world. The consistency of the self is dissolved into relations: intentionality in Husserl, being-in-the world or *Miteinandersein* in Heidegger, or continual renewal of *durée* in Bergson. Concrete reality is man always already in relation with the world, or always already projected beyond his instant. These relations cannot be reduced to theoretical representation. The latter would only confirm the autonomy of the thinking subject. In order to demolish the idea of the subject closed in upon itself, one must uncover, beneath objectification, very different relations that sustain it: man is in situation before situating himself. Not that belonging to being can be reduced to a place in the hierarchical universe, or to a function in a physical mechanism, without the involvement of any truth. But the relation with the object is not necessarily a relation with being, and objective knowledge is not the original itinerary of truth. Objective knowledge is already placed in a light that lights its own way. Light is needed to see the light. This requirement is not only that of the psalmist[2]—it is the philosophers' as well. In this sense, it signals that end of the propaedeutic and ontological privilege of a theory of knowledge that sets forth the manner in which a subject reaches the object. But it opens out upon a knowledge of being and a theory of that knowledge.

The knowledge of being does not maintain its claim to knowledge by imitating, in its own way, the relation to the object—in this case to a thicker, more impenetrable, or larger object than that of objective knowledge. Communication with being in original truth consists, first, in no longer focusing on being, in no longer being discourse *about* being. It is not thematization. It merely sketches out the locus within which any proposition about an object will have meaning. In Heidegger, the revelation of truth spreads only the first light, necessary to see light. We must respond to him before speaking of this. In Bergson's view, truth is decision, invention and creation rather the reflection of being.[3] Bergson's intuition is not only, beyond any exterior or lateral view of Being, a union with it. It is invention and creation in its very union. Truth, here, is the fundamental event of being itself.

Thus knowledge, if it is directed in contemporary philosophy beyond the object toward being, does not go to being with the same movement with which it goes to the object. How can this movement be described positively? Contemporary philosophy is in search of a theory of that ultimate knowledge. Buber's philosophy should be viewed from this angle.

3 Experience and Meeting

For Buber as for most contemporaries, the self is not a substance but a relation. It can only exist, as an *I*, as taking an interest in a *Thou* or as an *I* grasping an *It*. This is not the same

Blanchot's sphere? (not quite)

relation with two different terms. The relation itself, as the phenomenologists also maintain, relates to each of these terms in a different way.

The sphere of the *It* coincides with everything the *I* approaches in his or her objective and practical experience. Experience and practice are taken together (IT, 34), without consideration of the non-objectifying structure of practice in which the engagement of the self in being is presently viewed. For Buber as for Bergson, use is the most superficial relation, and coincides with the intellection of things. In fact the domain of the *It* is posited as the correlative of all our intellectual, voluntary and affective activities, but in the sense that these focus on an object. "I perceive something. I have the sensation of something. I represent something to myself. I think something. ... All this, and all that resembles it, together make up the domain of the *It*" (IT, 4). The *It* is here described in the same terms Husserl uses to designate the intentional object. Thus the *I–Thou*, to the extent that it differs from the *I–It*, designates a relation that is not an intentionality, and that, in Buber's thinking, conditions intentionality. And this is, well before Heidegger, but in agreement with Bergsonism, the attempt to find structures prior to those that constitute the objectifying intellect.

The human beings of which we speak in the third person ("he," "she," "they") and my own psychological states as well belong to the realm of the *It*. The *I* experiences these entities, exploring no more than their surfaces, not becoming engaged with them with his or her whole being (IT, 3), and not truly coming out of his or her self (IT, 5). *It* is neuter. The neuter suggests that, in the *It*, beings are not approached in the uniqueness by which they are other than all others. They are what is available, what by its mass counts for action. Since the true intention of knowing is directed toward what is independent, the totally *other* is not attained here. Being is assimilated, gives itself as needed in its anonymity of merchandise, in its past of "accumulated reserves," or in the instant of pleasure which is not a true present (IT, 12–13).

& the sphere of the It!

I–Thou: a relation that is not an intentionality

not Blanchot's Neutre

The *I–Thou* relation consists in placing oneself before an outside being, i.e. one who is radically *other*, and in recognizing that being as such. This recognition of alterity does not consist in forming an idea of alterity. Having an idea of something belongs to the realm of *I–It*. It is not a question of thinking the other person, or of thinking him or her as other—but of addressing that person as a *Thou*. The adequate access to the alterity of the other is not a perception, but this saying of *Thou*. There is immediate contact in this invocation, without there being an object. This is an original relation (IT, 18), the objective knowledge of which is but a deformation. It is not that the *Thou* is some new kind of object: rather the "movement" that meets the *Thou* does not resemble thematization. The beings thus addressed are ineffable, because I speak *to* them before speaking *of* them, and in speaking *of* them I have already broken off contact. Speaking *to* them is thus tantamount to letting their alterity be fulfilled. The *I–Thou* relation, then, appears from the outset to escape the gravitational field of the *I–It* in which the alleged exteriority of the object remains held.

The *I–Thou*, in which the "me" [le moi] is no longer the subject, is the Relation *par excellence*—the relation that transcends the limits of the Self (BM, 171–174) (though we may wonder, in Buber, what determines these limits). That relation is in the being of the *I*: when the *I* affirms itself fully, it is inconceivable without the *Thou* (IT, 11–28 *et passim*). The *Thou* as the sign of a dimension in which the *I* seeks, that is to say, has already found, a being that is other—the *Thou* as horizon of the meeting—is *a priori* or innate (IT, 27). The *I* finds itself in connection, without the connections being reducible to *thoughts,* which disconnect all connections. "It (the *I*) stands within a primal community with the whole of Being" (BM, 196). In primitive mentalities, the law of participation is, according to Buber, an indication of the original character of these connections—the primacy of *I–Thou* over *I–It* (IT, 18–22).

The difference between experience focusing *on* an object and the meeting that places one being *facing* another—a difference concerning the relation itself and not just the correlative terms; the richness of the analyses establishing that difference (which is developed in ways that Feuerbach, who formulated the *I–Thou*, did not foresee); and the desire to base experience on the meeting: these constitute Buber's fundamental contribution to the theory of knowledge. The fact that the relation with the being that underlies objective knowledge leads not to the inhuman and neuter entity, Heidegger's *Sein des Seienden*, but rather to a *Seiendes* that is the other person, and therefore to society as the first event of being: this seems to me to be of great spiritual importance.

Finally, let us note the phenomenological character of Buber's descriptions. They are set within the world of *perception*, the perspectives of which have no need of being justified by any intellectual authority. The non-theoretical modes of existence are "meaning-giving" and the ontological structures are never separable from them.

4 The Ontology of the Interval

The relation is not reducible to a "subjective" event, since the *I* does not represent the *Thou* to itself, but meets it. The meeting is distinguished from the relation which, according to Plato, the soul can have with itself in its silent discourse (BM, 50–51). The *I–Thou* meeting is not in the subject; it is in being (IT, 14–15). This does not mean that it takes place in front of the *I*. The ontological sphere is not a block of being, but event. The "between-the-two," the interval between the *I* and the *Thou*, the *Zwischen*, is the locus in which the very work of being takes place (IT, 14–15).

Nor is the interval a kind of interstellar space, existing independently from the *I* and the *Thou* that it separates. The dimension of the interval is accessible exclusively to the *I* and *Thou* of each particular meeting (BM, 205). Supreme transcendence is bound to the supreme particularity of the *I* and *Thou*. Buber does not only bring out a being that is differently constructed

than nature and things, as is the case, for example, of the
becoming-different of the Eleatics. The interval is no longer
separable from one's personal adventure: because of that personal
adventure it is more objective than any objectivity. The *Zwischen*
is recreated afresh in each meeting, and is ever new, as are the
instants of the Bergsonian *durée*.

But if the notion of the between-the-two functions as the
fundamental category of being, it is in man that its action
unfolds (BM, 203). Man is not a subject who constitutes: he is
the very articulation of the meeting. The human self is not a
being among beings, but a being who is a category, and who
since Nietzsche, according to Buber, has been recognized as
such (BM, 155). He is meeting. He is that which puts itself at a
distance (and already the anonymous existence of the world and
of things that have survived the use we make of them is
affirmed in that distancing) and he is at the same time the
entering into relations with that world which is distant—other.[4]
Through these two movements, man is at the center of being,
and all philosophy is anthropology. He is not at the center by
virtue of being a thinking subject, but in his totality, because his
totality is the concreteness of his situation. His totality sustains
his thought itself, and is already transcendence. "Only when we
try to understand the human person in his whole situation, in
the possibilities of his relation to all that is not himself, do we
understand man" (BM, 181). "It is not by a relation to oneself
but by a relation to another that man can be complete" (BM,
168).

Man, as the possibility of distance and relation, is not the
subject of Nature, but neither is he a part of it. To say that the
I–Thou relation is not psychological, but ontological, does not
mean reducing it to a *real* relation in nature. The interval in
which the game of being is played out, and which human existence both creates and bridges, implies the abandoning of the
notion of a content being, a realized being, a narrated being—
an abandonment that characterizes the entire ontology of our
time.

5 Liaison and Embrace

What is the structure of this meeting/knowing, which is also an ontological event?

The *I–Thou* relation is true knowledge because it maintains in its integrity the alterity of the *Thou*, instead of misunderstanding it in the anonymity of the *It*. It is noteworthy that the movement by which the *I* withdraws, distancing itself from the *Thou* and letting it be (as Heidegger would say), is the same movement that makes a liaison with the *Thou* possible. There is in fact no liaison worthy of the name except where there is otherness. Liaison, *Verbundenheit*, is, so to speak, the very manifestation of otherness (IT, 24–25). The presence of the *Thou*, the Other, is *ipso facto* addressed to me, requiring a response. "He who ceases to make a response ceases to hear the Word" (BM, 45). It is impossible to remain the spectator of the *Thou*, because his or her existence as a *Thou* is the word that *Thou* addresses to me. And only a being responsible for another can be in dialogue with that other. This responsibility, in the etymological sense of the term, is not the verbal exchange, but the *dialogue* in which the meeting is achieved. The impossibility of remaining a spectator does not come from a practical and tragic involvement in a situation not of my choosing: it is not an unhappy fate, but the necessity of responding to the word. A non-human reality that concerns me is a reality that speaks to me (BM, 9–10) and the "that speaks to me,"[5] used in this way, is not a metaphor. It expresses the very essence of language.

Truth, instead of presenting itself to an impassible subject, looking down upon the real, is a committed involvement [*engagement*] rendered all the more inevitable by the fact that truth lets the other remain in his or her alterity. While the knowing being was unable to reach the absolute in total detachment (the impossibility of total detachment, in Plato's *Parmenides,* is what separated being from truth)—in Buber's conception, committed engagement gives us access to alterity. Exterior and other is that which can commit us to a responsibility (BM, 45).

Buber's project consists in maintaining, in the *I–Thou* relation, the radical alterity of the *Thou*, specifically in liaison. The *I* does not absorb the *Thou* as an object, nor is it absorbed by the *Thou* ecstatically. The *I–Thou* relation is a relation with what remains absolute despite the relation. Parmenides' problem of truth is resolved in the social relationship.

The committed involvement in question is strictly individual. Truth is not reflection on committed involvement, but that involvement itself. The human being *qua* category is each man (BM, 138) and not man-in-general, which would be accessible through the *I–It* relation. Here we encounter one of the themes of the philosophy of existence. This extreme particularizing of existence is presented not as a form of relativism, but as the ground of knowledge (BM, 124).

But knowledge through concerned involvement is not coincidence with being, as opposed to the representation of being, as in Bergsonism or in certain claims of the philosophy of existence. In order to know pain, "the mind casts itself into the depth of this real pain" (BM, 192), rather than contemplating it as an onlooker, and that is true of "all the events of the soul, which are more like mysteries than spectacles, and whose meaning remains closed to those who do not let themselves participate" (BM, 192). But even for the privileged example of pain, which assumes a simple coincidence, Buber requires a liaison of a different order, dialogical in nature: a communication with "the pain of the world" (BM, 192–193).

The liaison of responsibility and dialogue, which is the original relation with being or knowledge, is reciprocal. But is that reciprocity not concluded or deduced? The ultimate essence of the dialogue is manifested in a structure Buber calls *Umfassung* (embrace), and which is certainly one of the most original. In the *I–Thou*, the reciprocity of the relation is somehow lived directly, not just known. The *I* in its relationships with the *Thou* relates to itself through the *Thou*—relates to the *Thou* as to someone who relates to the *I*, as if brushing against the skin of the *Thou*. A return to self through the *Thou*. This

embrace

must be distinguished from the psychological phenomenon of *Einfühlung*, in which the subject puts itself in the other's place, forgetting itself. In *Einfühlung*, the *I* forgets itself as the *Thou* of the *Thou*, whereas all the acuity of the *Umfassung* resides in the *I*'s actuality (BM, 97).

6 Truth

Verbundenheit resides in the reciprocity of the *I–Thou*, in the dialogue in which I involve myself concernfully with the *Thou*, precisely because absolutely other. The essence of the word [*parole*] does not, then, initially consist in its signification and narrative power, but in the response it elicits. The word is not true because the thought it states corresponds to the thing, or reveals being. It is true when it proceeds from the *I–Thou* relation, which is the ontological process itself. It is true when it accomplishes the reciprocity of the relation by eliciting the response and instituting the single person uniquely capable of responding. The static notion of truth, which is to be that which reappears as long as the truth can be said, is destroyed in this conception. In opposition to immutable being we have not only the being-becoming of Heraclitus or Bergson, which cannot be expressed by a word because the word [*mot*] immobilizes. Buber describes a being no narration could grasp, because that being is living dialogue between beings who do not relate to one another as contents: *one being has nothing to say about the other*. The acuity of the *I–Thou* relation is in the total *formalism of that relation*. To perceive a content in the other person would already be to relate to him or her as to an object—to enter into the *I–It*.

The notion of truth (for which Buber uses language that is not sufficiently didactic) is determined by the *I–Thou* as the fundamental relation with being. We must distinguish between truth *qua* possessed, an impersonal result, also called truth of knowledge (BM, 99), and truth of being, which is, for a reality, the fact of truly being, and *which designates God*. But truth also

[handwritten marginalia: "The essence of the word"; "does it?"; "Truth of knowledge v. truth of being"]

means "a real attitude toward being," "*Realverhältnis zum Seienden*" (BM, 47), correlative to the proof that verifies it (*Bewährung*). "To know means, for us creatures, fulfilling our relation toward being, each one his or her own, in truth [*wahrhaft*] and in full responsibility, in welcoming its entire manifestation faithfully, with an open mind, open to the world, and incorporating it into our way of being; this is the way in which the living truth surges forth and endures" (BM, 99).

Citing Kierkegaard, Buber says that the particular verifies the truth by the fact "of expressing what has been said [*das Gesagte*] by personal existence"; this makes truth not a correspondence with being, but the correlative of an authentic life. But Buber, at this point, corrects the quoted text. "I would almost have said," he writes, "the particular verifies the truth by the fact of express-ing the unsaid [*das Ungesagte*] by personal existence" (BM, 48). Thus Buber clearly removes from truth its essence of spoken word or content of any sort. Truth is entirely attitude, a seeking after, or a struggle for, truth. Henceforth truth means far more the authenticity of a life than the agreement between appearance and being: "*eine menschliche Wahrheit, die Wahrheit menschlicher Existenz*" [a human truth, the truth of human existence] (BM, 106). Perhaps "living truth", the expression so frequently used by Buber, is not a romantic term but refers to an existence that is determined by the authentic and the inauthentic rather than by a true idea.

And yet, in the responsibility that links the *I* to the *Thou*, it is the "search for truth" that authenticates the personality of the *I* and tears it away from the bonds of an anonymous collectivity and the depths of the unconscious, for which it would function simply as a mouthpiece (BM 79ff). Through the search after truth, the *I–Thou* involvement becomes a personal involvement. But at this point does truth not take on its theoretical and intel-lectualist physiognomy once again? And do we not catch a glimpse, in the *I–Thou* without which the *I* cannot be, of a superseded subjectivity?

7 The Formalism of the Meeting

The *I–Thou* relation accomplishes nothing but the meeting. The *Thou* had no attribute to which the *I* might aspire, or that it might know. The privileged examples of the relation are chosen in *Zwiesprache* [conversation between two people] between beings who do not know each other (BM, 3). "Between the I and the Thou, there are no conceptual structures, there is no prescience, no fantasy ... no goal, no desire, no anticipation. Every means is an obstacle. It is only when all means disappear that the meeting takes place" (IT, 11–12). The content would, in Buber's view, be mediation, and would compromise the directness and simplicity of the act. Buber uses the term *geschehen* [to happen] (BM, 3) to designate that nameless event, the purity of the act of transcendence, the transparent activity, so to speak, of that event. Every meeting is a unique event that cannot be told, that cannot be joined together with other presents to make up a *story*. It is a pure spark, like Bergson's instant of intuition (BM, 69), like the "almost nothing" of his disciple Jankélévitch, in which the relation of consciousness to a content thins to that limit at which consciousness no longer has a content, but is left like the point of a needle penetrating being. The relation is a fulguration of instants without continuity, which refuses to be a continuous, owned existence (IT, 109; BM, 65, 108). Perhaps this way of seeing things is also related to Buber's religious liberalism—his religiosity which stands opposed to religion, and leads him, in reacting against the fixed, rigid forms of a spiritual dogmatism, to place contact above its content, and the pure, unqualifiable presence of God above all dogma and rule. But the question remains open as to whether transcendence, without becoming a relation with a content and dogmas, may not be qualified by the dimension of height or lowliness—a dimension upon which it opens *qua* relation. But as we shall see, the ethical elements of the *I–Thou*, which abound in Buber's descriptions, are not decisive. The *I–Thou* is possible in relation to things.

Although Buber gives privileged status to the interhuman *I–Thou*, as being the case in which reciprocity can blossom forth in language, he also gives consideration to the meeting as a relation to God and to things. We can conduct ourselves toward God as if we were called (IT, 6). The tree, rather than serving me or dissolving into representations, can face me in person, speak to me and elicit a response. For Husserl, the presentation of the thing as a living body was but one mode of representation.[6] For Buber, the presentation of the thing as person breaks away from representation, and binds me. In this case, the thing is not given, for I am also to a degree bound by it. The bond is reciprocal (IT, 8, 15, 33 *et passim*). The thing that is simply given, and that I dominate, is in the realm of the *It*. The way in which the artist meets the thing, in creating a work of art, is one of the ways of responding to the meeting.

In one of Buber's last essays, "Man and his Image-Work,"[7] the sensible world that is available for our use and needs, the world of the *It*, is itself *conditioned* by the meeting that originally typified the interhuman *I–Thou*, or even the *I–Thou* that connects us to God and nature. Sense perception, which is the source of all human behavior (KM, 156), is not a subjective reality *within* man. It is man's response to meeting X, the scientific object that, unrepresentable, awaits man (KM, 158). Man's response is the vision that gives form (*Schau*). "This *Schau* is a form-giving faithfulness to the unknown that does its work in collaboration with it. This faithfulness is not manifested in the phenomenon but in the inaccessible being with which we find ourselves in communication" (KM, 159). Here, the psychology of form (*Gestaltpsychologie*) is used. But Buber does not go back to the constitution of things from sensations: the elaboration of which he speaks takes place within the *Zwischen* [the interval]. Only the *Zwischen* itself belongs to being that is neither a subject nor an object. Buber had already said this in *I and Thou* (IT, 94): "The constitution of the world and the disappearance of the world are not within me, nor are they outside me; they cannot be said to *be* at all: they continually happen [*Geschehen*] and their occurring is dependent upon my own life." In "Man and His Image-Work," Buber includes the meeting in the being of nature, in which, consequently, perception does its work in the same way as the other actions in life. "Man is not a part of nature solely by his vital actions and as a being capable of *sui generis* movement, but also as a perceiving being. My perception, without negating the spirituality of subjective existence, is an act of the natural order, of which we are a part, both myself and the X" (KM, 158). "Nature aspires to integrity, and that means to the state of being perceived" (ibid.).

Nature, understood in this way (and this may be the essential lesson in this conception), is neither a subjective appearance nor an objective realm. Both are *abstractions*. The true concept of being is in the meeting between beings that are, by themselves, still abstract; thus, the sensible world is more objective than any objectivity, and perception is the original event of being. Or, to put it another way, being is event.

It is quite characteristic, however, of Buber's theory of knowledge that a common measure exists between the relation to things and the relation to man. That is why the responsibility we have found underlying language itself will never take on a strictly ethical meaning, since the response of the self to the X of perception is, in an imperfect form (KM, 162ff), what the *I–Thou* relation will become. The interhuman relation, with the ethical resonance it takes on—but which in Buber it takes on through the interposition and imitation of God, and through a theology too well informed on the nature of God (BM, 56–57; 60–61)—is a special case of the meeting. Buber does recognize a surpassing of the perceptual meeting in four forms: knowledge, love, art and belief. But these four forms cannot be deduced, in their specificity, from the *I–Thou* relation. Is there a vacillation here in Buber's thought? Although he admits, from the publication of *I and Thou* on, that things can belong to the *I–Thou* relation, yet the interhuman relation, once the *Thou* has a human face, is not only privileged but *conditions* all the others. "All the rest lives in *his* light" (IT, 8). "And one can have confidence in the world because this person exists" (BM, 98). The light of the *Thou*, like Plato's intelligible sun (the idea of the Good) that preceded it, or like Heidegger's phosphorescence of "the Being of beings" that came later, would then constitute the original truth to which all other truth harks back.

8   A Few Objections

How can we maintain the specificity of the interhuman *I–Thou* without bringing out the strictly ethical meaning of responsibility, and how can we bring out the ethical meaning without questioning the reciprocity on which Buber always insists? Doesn't the ethical begin when the *I* perceives the *Thou* as higher than itself?

We shall direct our main criticism to the reciprocity of the *I–Thou* relation. Ethical themes are frequent in Buber's own descriptions, but a more abstract structure of distance and relation also replaces the *I–Thou* relation, and apparently even underlies the *I–It* relation. We wonder whether the relation with the alterity of others which appears in the form of dialogue, of question and answer, can be described without introducing a paradoxical difference of level between the *I* and the *Thou*. The originality of the *I–Thou* comes from the fact that that relation is known not from the outside, but from the *I* who brings it about. Its place is therefore not interchangeable with the place occupied by the *Thou*. In what does this position of ipseity consist? If the *I* becomes *I* in saying *Thou*, I have obtained this position from my correlate, and the *I–Thou* relation is like all other relations: as if an external onlooker were speaking of *I* and *Thou* in the third person. The meeting, which is formal, can be reversed, read from left to right just as well as from right to left. In the ethics in which the other is at once higher and poorer than I, the *I* is distinguished from the *Thou*, not by any sort of "attributes," but by the dimension of height, which breaks with Buber's formalism. The primacy of the other, and his nakedness and destitution, do not qualify the purely formal relation with its otherness: they already qualify this otherness itself.

Thus the relation itself is something other than that empty contact, always to be renewed, the culmination of which is a totally spiritual friendship (BM, 100–101). The recurrence of these themes of angelic spiritualism (fortunately counterbalanced by superlative pages on the relationship between the *I–Thou* and the crowd, in opposition to the views of Kierkegaard and Heidegger, and a correction of earlier texts that placed the "they" in the *It*), expressed in an intermittently spiritualist and edifying language, seem to us today the most dated elements of a work otherwise so rich. This pure spiritualism of friendship, like the simple materialism of objective contact, seems to us not to be in keeping with the phenomena. Buber rises in violent opposition to Heidegger's notion of *Fürsorge*—or care given to others—which would be, for the German philosopher, the true access to others (BM, 169–170). It is not, surely, to Heidegger that one should turn for instruction in the love of man or social justice. But *Fürsorge*, as a response to essential destitution, is a mode of access to the otherness of the Other. It does justice to that dimension of height and of human distress, by which (far more than by *Umfassung*) the Relation is characterized. We may well ask ourselves whether clothing the naked and feeding the hungry are not the true and concrete access to the otherness of the other person—more authentic than the ether of friendship. Is dialogue possible without *Fürsorge*? If I criticize Buber for extending the *I–Thou* to things, it is not because he seems to be animistic in his relation to nature; it is rather that he seems too much the *artiste* in his relation to people.

The transition from the subject/object relation to the I–Thou relation is also the movement of consciousness into that new sphere of existence: the interval, the between, the *Zwischen*. Buber forcefully asserts the radical difference between the soul's silent dialogue with itself and the real dialogue with the other (BM, 50–51). But is it not in consciousness, after all, that the *Zwischen* manifests its structures? Reciprocity and *Umfassung* [inclusion] are, in fact, the *dialoguization* of all states of consciousness: its entry into the sphere of the *Zwischen* (BM, 97). But Buber allows himself to say: "All dialogue draws its authenticity from consciousness of the element of *Umfassung*" (ibid.). Consciousness reappears behind *Umfassung*. A theory of ontological knowledge directed toward the understanding of the being that crosses the "space" of the in-between must show how the Relation by itself, apart from its goal, differs from knowledge. It must show how that space bends, transforms, or inverts the very movement of consciousness and knowledge, if it is true that in the end everything is said in terms of knowledge, and the *I–It* corrodes the *I–Thou* (IT, 33–34).

This leads us to a question that concerns more than just Buber's philosophy. What sort of knowledge makes up the theory of knowledge itself? The question arises for any epistemology that places the origin of truth in an activity or an existence other than the theoretical activity in which the truth about truth is at least presented and exposited—i.e. epistemology itself. For of the theoretical nature of philosophy itself there can be no doubt. But is this characteristic simply the result of the technique of teaching? Perhaps it only reflects the philosopher's return to the Cave, where he is forced to use the language of slaves in chains.[8] If so, to philosophize would be to live in a certain way, and, according to Buber's teachings, to practice (perhaps better than others) the dialogue with the real—as an artist, a friend, or a believer. But isn't philosophy an attitude distinct from all others? Isn't *philosophari* essentially something different from *vivere*? And isn't the theory of knowledge we have just described—that truth about truth—obtained by means of an intellectual process [*une démarche spirituelle*] that is no longer dialogical? Or if it is still dialogue, is it not of a new kind, in which we see not the concern for the *Relation* but the desire to obtain independence for the *I*, even if it be a bound (*verbunden*) *I*? Perhaps philosophy is defined by a break with participation in totality; and that is why it is theory, i.e. critique. Let us not dwell, here, on Buber's indifference toward theoretical knowledge, which he associates with the primary word *I–It*, and classes too hastily together with the visual relations with being, without ever expressing himself on the significance of physico-mathematical knowledge. Yet, as a prelude to critique, theoretical knowledge is of importance for the primary words (*Urworte*) themselves. Buber, who articulated with such penetration the Relation and the distancing that makes it possible, did not take separation seriously. Man is not just the category of distance and meeting, he is also a separate being. He accomplishes that isolation in a process of subjectification that is not just the recoil from the word *Thou*. Buber does not give expression to the movement, distinct from distancing and the relation, in which the *I* emerges from the self. It is impossible for man to forget his metamorphosis of subjectivity.

3 Dialogue with Martin Buber

The following is the restoration of a dialogue. From the book published by Kohlhammer in Stuttgart in 1963 (in a series entitled "Philosophen des 20. Jahrhunderts") in which my essay "Martin Buber and the Theory of Knowledge" appeared in German, I excerpt the response Buber was good enough to give to my objection. [i.e. the objection contained in Levinas's essay; see above, 32–35]. I sent him a letter, to which he responded with only a few polite words. They were handwritten, beneath a printed text that Buber sent (in 1963) to all those who had greeted him on his eighty-fifth birthday. That text has never been published. I do so here, because of its intrinsic beauty.

May the reader see no presumption on my part in publishing my own letter. It merely contributes to clarifying the critical attitude I take up with respect to the essential problem of philosophy posed by Buber. It goes without saying that I do not take the few couteous words he wrote in response as an expression of agreement. Especially now that the Discourtesy par excellence has occurred, its great silence covering over the interruption in our recent dialogue.[1]

Buber's Response

Levinas is quite mistaken in assuming that, for me, the *I–Thou* relation culminates in "a purely spiritual friendship." On the contrary, that relation appears to me to reach its greatness and authentic energy when two human beings not very akin to one another spiritually, who belong rather to different, even opposing, spiritual families, face one another in such a way that even in the course of the sharpest controversy, one of them knows, focuses on, identifies, recognizes, accepts and confirms the other as that particular person; in such a way that each one, in the common situation in which he finds himself (even if the commonality of the situation is that of the struggle in which they face each other), imagines the experience that the adversary has of that same situation, the manner in which he lives it, the whole psychic process peculiar to him. No friendship here! It is the fellow feeling of the human creature fulfilling itself. No "ether," as Levinas thinks, but the hard earth of men, the *common* in the *non-common*.

Levinas opposes me by praising "solicitude for the Other" (*Fürsorge*), which, according to him, gives access to the otherness of the Other. Experience seems to me to teach the following: He who has that access without the caring [*sollicitude*] will find it again also in caring; he who is devoid of that access will clothe the naked and feed the hungry in vain. He will not utter a true "Thou" without great difficulty. Not until everyone has been clothed and fed will the true ethical problem become visible.

My Letter of March 11, 1963

Most revered Mr. Buber,

I have just been sent a copy of the German edition of the lovely volume dedicated to you, in which I had the honor of collaborating. I am pleased with, and proud of, this new homage paid you by the entire thinking Western world.

I am also happy to congratulate you on the occasion of your jubilee.[2] My best wishes for your health and the continuation of your work.

Among your responses to objectors, I find a page concerning myself. Allow me to comment.

It has never been my opinion that the mechanical act of providing food and clothing constituted by itself the fact of the meeting between I and Thou. My ideas on that subject are not, after all, that simplistic. I think that the *Du sagen* [Saying Thou] is already, *ipso facto*, a giving. Once the *Du sagen* has been separated from this giving, even if it is established between strangers, it is a "purely spiritual," ethereal friendship, i.e. already enervated, as it may become in a certain social milieu. That the *Du sagen* operates immediately and already through my body (including my giving hands), that it therefore presupposes my body (as lived body), things (as objects of enjoyment) and the Other's hunger, that the *Sagen* is thus embodied, i.e. beyond the organs of speech or song or artistic activity, that the Other is always, *qua* Other, the poor and destitute one (while at the same time being my lord), and that the relation is thus *essentially* dissymmetrical: such are the thoughts that were behind my "objection." They remain within the good Biranian tradition.[3] But I also think that when Rabbi Johanan said, in *Sanhedrin*, "*gedolah legimah*,"[4] he was not just making a plea for the philanthropic idea of public soup kitchens for the poor. I also think that *giving* is not the same thing as *giving oneself*, as the *hahamim*[5] perceived when they said that "*bekol meodehah*"[6] means *money* and that money is sometimes more (and in any case different) than giving one's soul and one's life.

I apologize for my prolixity, but I owed these lines to my veneration of you and your work.

Again let me express my great respect and good wishes.

Buber's Reply (postmarked April, 1963)

Once again the hour for uncommon gratitude has come for me. I have much to give thanks for. For me, this was a time to meditate once more upon the word *thank [remercier]*. Its ordinary meaning is generally understood, but it does not lend itself to a description that would define it unequivocally.

One sees immediately that it belongs to that category of words whose original meaning is multiple. Thus it awakens a variety of associations in various languages.

In German and English, the verb for "*remercier*," which is *danken* and *thank*, is related to *denken* and *think*, in the sense of *having in one's thoughts*, remembering someone. The person who says "I thank you," "*Ich danke dir*," assures the other person that he or she will be kept in the memory, and more specifically in the good memory, that of friendship and joy.[7] It is significant that the eventuality of a different sort of memory doesn't arise.

It is otherwise in Hebrew. The verb form *hodot* means first *to come in support of someone*, and only later, *to thank*. He who thanks someone rallies in support of the one thanked. He will now—and from now on—be his ally. This includes, to be sure, the idea of memory, but implies more. The fact occurs not only within the soul: it proceeds from there toward the world, to become act and event. Now, to come in support of someone in this way is to confirm him in his existence.

I propose to vow a thankful memory and to come in support of all who have sent me their good wishes for my eighty-fifth birthday.

Jerusalem, February, 1963

The following words were handwritten:

I thank you especially for the explanations contained in your letter.[8]

Martin Buber

4 Paul Celan: From Being to the Other

For Paul Ricoeur

... all things are less than
they are,
all are more.

(Paul Celan)

Toward the Other

"I cannot see any basic difference," Paul Celan wrote to Hans
Bender, "between a handshake and a poem." There is the poem,
the height of language, reduced to the level of an interjection, a
form of expression as undifferentiated as a wink, a sign to one's
neighbor! A sign of what? Of life, of goodwill? Of complicity?
Or a sign of nothing, or of complicity for no reason: a saying
without a said. Or is it a sign that is its own signified: the subject
signals that sign-giving to the point of becoming a sign through
and through. An elementary communication without revelation,
stammering infancy of discourse, a most clumsy intrusion in the
famous "*language* that speaks," the famous "*die Sprache spricht*":
entrance of the beggar into "the house of being."

The fact is that Paul Celan (whom Heidegger was somehow
able, nonetheless, to extoll during one of the former's stays in

Germany)[1] tells us of his lack of understanding for a certain language that institutes the world in being, signifying like the radiance of the *physis* of the pre-Socratics; since Celan compares a language with a "road" that is "so beautiful" in the mountains,

> where, on the left the Turk's-cap lily blooms like nowhere else, and on the right the rampion, and where *dianthus superbus*, maiden-pink, rises not far away ... a language not for you and not for me— for I ask for whom was it conceived then, the earth, it was not for you I say that it was conceived and not for me—a language of for ever, without *I* and without *You*, nothing but *He*, nothing but *It*, do you see, nothing but *She*, and that's all.[2]

An impersonal language.[3]

The fact is, then, that for Celan the poem is situated precisely at that pre-syntactic and (as is surely *de rigueur* these days!) pre-logical level, but a level also pre-disclosing: at the moment of pure touching, pure contact, grasping, squeezing—which is, perhaps, a way of giving, right up to and including the hand that gives. A language of proximity for proximity's sake, older than that of "the truth of being"—which it probably carries and sustains—the first of the languages, response preceding the question, responsibility for the neighbor, by its *for the other*, the whole marvel of giving.

The poem "moves in one bound out in front of that other whom it presumes reachable, able to be set free, vacant perhaps." Around that statement in *The Meridian*,[4] a text is built, in which Celan gives us what he is able to perceive of his poetic act. An elliptic, allusive text, constantly interrupting itself in order to let through, in the interruptions, his other voice, as if two or more discourses were on top of one other, with a strange coherence, not that of a dialogue, but woven in a counterpoint that consti-tutes—despite their immediate melodic unity—the texture of his poems. But *The Meridian*'s vibrant formulas require interpre-tation.

The poem goes toward the other. It hopes to find him freed and vacant. The poet's solitary work of chiseling the precious matter of words[5] is the act of "driving a vis-à-vis out from behind his cover." The poem "becomes dialogue, is often an impassioned dialogue,[6] ... meetings, paths of a voice toward a vigilant Thou"[7]—Buber's categories! Would they, then, be preferred to so much brilliant exegesis majestically descending from the mysterious *Schwarzwald* upon Hölderlin, Trakel and Rilke, portraying poetry as opening the world, the place between earth and sky? Could it be that they are preferred to the storage of structures in the interstellar space of Objectivity? That uncertainty, the good or bad luck of being so stored, is scarcely felt by poets in Paris—who, however, are committed heart and soul to the same structural objectivity. Poetics of the avant-garde, in which the poet has no personal destiny. To them, Buber is preferred, without a doubt. The personal is the poetry of the poem: "the poem speaks! Of the date that is its own ... of the unique circumstance that properly concerns it."[8] The personal: from myself to the other. But Paul Celan's breathless meditation—daring to cite Malebranche from a text of Walter Benjamin's on Kafka and Pascal, according to Leon Chestov—obeys no norm. We must listen to him more closely: the poem that spoke of me speaks of "*that which concerns another; someone entirely other*"; it already speaks "with" another, "with another" who would even be close, "very close"; it "moves in one bound out in front of that 'other',"[9] already we are "far outside," already "in the clearness *of utopia.*[10] Poetry is ahead of us. La poésie, elle aussi, brûle nos étapes."[11]

Transcendence

The movement thus described goes from place to the non-place, from here to utopia. That there is, in Celan's essay on the poem, an attempt to think transcendence, is obvious.[12] *Poetry—conversion into the infinite of pure mortality and the dead letter.*[13] The paradox is not only in the infinite adventure of a dead letter; it is in the antimony in which the concept of transcendence itself unfolds—a leap over the chasm opened in being, to whom the very identity of the leaper inflicts a refutation. Is it not necessary to die, in order to transcend against nature and even against being? Or both to leap and not leap? Or does the poem perhaps allow the "I" to separate from itself? In Celan's terms: discover "a place in which the person, in grasping himself as a stranger to himself, emerges."[14] And does the poem that goes toward the other, "*turning, facing* him," postpone its ecstasy, "become more intense" in the interim, and in Celan's so ambiguous language, "persist at the limit of itself"? And does the poem, in order to last, adjourn its acumen, or in Celan's terms, "revoke itself ... carry itself over continually in order to last from its 'already-no-longer' to its 'still-here'?" But for this still-here the poet does not retain, in his passage to the other, his proud sovereignty of creator. In Celan's terms: the poet speaks "from the angle of orientation of his existence, and from the angle of orientation in which the creature declares himself. ... He who writes it [the poem] remains dedicated to it."[15] A singular de-substantiation of the *I*. To make oneself completely into a sign, perhaps that is it.[16] Enough of those glorious imitations of a creator! "Stop pestering us with the *poiein* and other nonsense," Celan writes to Hans Bender. A gesture of recognition of the other, a handshake, a saying without a said—these things are important by their interpellation rather than by their message; important by their attention! "Attention, like a pure prayer of the soul," of which Malebranche speaks, in so many unexpected echoes from Walter Benjamin's pen: extreme receptivity, but extreme donation; attention—a mode of consciousness without distraction, i.e. without the power of escape through dark underground passages; full illumination, projected not in order to see ideas, but in order to prohibit evasion; the first meaning of that insomnia that is conscience—rectitude of responsibility before any appearance of forms, images, or things.

Things will indeed appear, the said of this poetic saying, but in the movement that carries them toward the other, as figures of this movement. "All things, all beings, as they journey toward the other, will be figures, for the poem, of that other. ... Around me who calls out and gives it a name it can gather." The centrifugal movement of the *for the other*—might it be the mobile axis of being? Or its rupture? Or its meaning? The fact of speaking to the other—the poem—precedes all thematization; it is in that act that qualities gather themselves into things. But the poem thus leaves the real its alterity, which pure imagination tears away from it; the poem "lets otherness's ownmost also speak: the time of the other."[17]

The going out toward the other man, is it a going out? "A step outside of man—but into a sphere directed toward the human—excentric."[18] As if humanity were a genus allowing within its logical space (its extension) an absolute break; as if in going toward the other man we transcended the human, toward utopia. And as if utopia were not the dream and the lot of an accursed wandering, but the "clearing" in which man shows himself: "light of utopia. ... And man? And the creature?—In such light."[19]

In the Light of Utopia

This unusual outside is not another landscape. Beyond the mere strangeness of art and the openness of beings on being,[20] the poem takes yet another step: strangeness is the stranger, the neighbor. Nothing is more strange or foreign than the other man, and it is in the light of utopia that man shows himself. Outside all enrootedness and all dwelling: statelessness as authenticity!

But the surprise of that adventure, in which the *I* dedicates himself to the other in the non-place, is the return. Not return as a response of the one who is called, but by the circularity of this movement that does not turn back, the circularity of this perfect trajectory, this meridian that, in its finality without end, describes the poem. It is as if in going toward the other I met myself and implanted myself in a land, henceforth native, and I were stripped of all the weight of my identity. A native land owing nothing to enrootedness, nothing to first occupation; a native land owing nothing to birth. A native, or a promised, land? Does it vomit out its inhabitants when they forget the circular journey that made that land familiar to them, and their wanderings, which were not for a change of scenery, but for de-paganization?[21] But habitation justified by movement toward the other is essentially Jewish.

In Celan's writings, Judaism is not a picturesque particularism or a family folklore. Clearly, in the eyes of this poet, Israel's Passion under Hitler (the theme of the twenty pages of "Strette" in *Strette*, a lament of laments, admirably translated by Jean Daive) had a significance for humanity *tout court*, of which Judaism is an extreme possibility—or impossibility. This is a break with the naivety of the Herald, the Messenger or the Shepherd of Being. Dehiscence of the world which offers, to get through the night, not a resting-place, but stones against which the beggar's staff strikes, reverberating in mineral language. Insomnia in the bed of being, the impossibility of curling up and forgetting oneself. Expulsion out of the *worldliness of the world*, nakedness of him who borrows all he owns; insensibility to nature, "for the Jew, as you very well know, what does he own that really belongs to him, that wasn't loaned, borrowed, never given back?" Here we are again on the mountain between the Turk's-cap lily and the rampion. Two Jews are there, or one Jew tragically divided against himself. "But they, first cousins, lack eyes," or, more precisely, a veil covers the appearance of all objects, "for the Jew and nature are two, have always been two, even today, even here ... poor Turk's-cap lily, poor rampion! ... poor things, you are not standing, not blossoming, and July is not July." And these mountains in their imposing massiveness? What of these mountains, of which Hegel said, with submission and freedom: "Thus it is"? Celan writes:

> The earth has folded up here, once and twice and thrice, and opened in the middle, and in the middle there is water, and the water is green and the green is white and the white comes from even farther up, from the glaciers.[22]

Above and beyond this silence and meaninglessness of a folding of earth called mountain, and in order to interrupt the sound of the staff striking against the stones and the reverberation of this noise against the cliffs, what is needed—as opposed to "the language in use here"—is a true speech.

For Celan also (in a world Mallarmé would not, however, have been able to imagine) the poem is the spiritual act *par excellence*. An act at once inevitable and impossible because of an "absolute poem that does not exist." The absolute poem does not say the meaning of being; it is not a variation on Hölderlin's *dichterisch wohnet der Mensch auf der Erde* [man dwells poetically on the earth]. It speaks the defection of all dimension; it goes toward utopia, "along the impossible path of the Impossible."[23] More and less than being. "The absolute poem: no, indeed, it does not, cannot exist."[24] Is Celan evoking the ideality of the unrealizable? That would be a gratuitous and facile interpretation that it would be difficult to justify. Does he not suggest a modality other than those situated between the limits of being and non-being? Does he not suggest poetry itself as an unheard-of modality of the *otherwise than being*? The Meridian: "like speech, immaterial, yet of the earth."[25] "From the least presumptuous poem ... that questioning that cannot be eluded, that unheard-of presumption."[26] The ineluctable: the interruption in the playful order of the beautiful and the play of concepts, and the *play of the world*; interrogation of the Other, a seeking for the Other. A seeking, dedicating itself to the other in the form of the poem. A chant rises in the giving, the one-for-the-other, the signifying of signification. A signification older than ontology and the thought of being, and that is presupposed by knowledge and desire, philosophy and libido.

5 Jeanne Delhomme: Penelope, or Modal Thought

Whether true knowledge is taken to be the conformity of ideas with the (sensible or suprasensible) real, or whether, more originarily, it is considered the manifestation[1] of being, which transforms itself into thought, and even man, and even human history, culture, or technology—the vocation of philosophy is taken to be tied to being. But does not that vocation, which heralds the emancipation from opinion and dogma, become fixed into a destiny? To be redeemed at the price of an allegiance to being—does this not amount to a change of dogmatisms and subservience? Belief in conformism and belief in evidence would seem to betray philosophical freedom, by subordinating themselves to history and being. Philosophy could only be philosophy in the form of a lightning bolt—or a storm—of disbelief, or as an always unheard-of modality of a language that undoes (in the intervals that separate the days) the weaving of ontologies.

The problem arises, even if an attachment stretching *beyond being* could emerge without history's chains; even if the *beyond* could avoid condensing too quickly into being, as happens in the case of the theologians' supernatural. If the reality of being, equaling itself in knowledge, were to be successfully freed of its weight, still, nothing would be frank or free in the ponderous civilizations that disclose and manage being, in the age-old or permanent dream of escape, in pessimism, which, though worn, finds new accents, and constitutes the most sincere part of existentialism, even now as it is passing out of fashion.

In Jeanne Delhomme's view, the conformity of thought with being (and even coincidence with the not-yet-constituted real, in Bergsonian intuition) is but the letter of the systems. In none of them is the spirit captured. Philosophy, in spirit and in truth, frees itself from the letter, from both conformity and conformism, and explodes massive being into a multiplicity of meanings in which the intelligence does its work. "There is nothing to believe." Philosophy is freedom, the polar opposite of life, morality, science, art and history. A proud freedom, but forlorn, being disillusionment. But to be disillusioned is not a passing mood: it is precisely the hard work of intelligent thought. It is an act of escape, an exceptional act, since in this case, paradoxically, the accomplishment does not end up in being, but *realizes*, so to speak, *the possible*; it ends up, not at all in the nonactualized potential of the germ, nor in the abstract idea, but in an ever fecund multiplicity of meanings that arise within meaning. Neither the negativity of abstraction nor that of the imagination is sufficiently negative to attain this extremity. As for the intentionality of consciousness that finds or invents its object, it would be, in this view, dogmatism itself: even by an object still forming itself within it, intentionality is supported as if the object were completed. Intentionality, the taking over of the conscious act by its object, whether encountered or constituted (which is perhaps the original event of history), would be precisely the modality of thought that subordinates the possible to being, and consequently sacrifices the possible *qua* possible. The thought of being becomes the being of thought. The genitive of intentionality is reversed. Historical continuity resumes, despite the ideality of the intentional object. Every attitude of consciousness changes into consciousness of the attitude, which passes into being, causes much ado, and becomes history.[2]

The search for an *epoche*, which, from one perspective, resembles Husserl's phenomenological reduction, would thus be impossible in consciousness! Would not the polarity of consciousness and being explain the role of history in Western philosophy, the definition of man by the understanding of being, and the ultimateness of the ontological problem? At least in philosophy considered as posited or stated in function of its sources and the influence it exerts—in which the coherent tapestry of effective, continuous, historical reason is woven.

Philosophy, as an act of intelligence and genius, plays itself out in an element other than consciousness or according to a modality other than intentionality.[3] That element is language. *In terms of* duration, a saying is said that is taken for discourse *on* duration; *in terms of* negativity a saying is said that is taken for discourse *on* negativity. In language, thought thinks itself *in terms of* ... rather than the terms being thought in language; the terms are thus categories rather than concepts. The *manner* of thought in saying (the modality) is the event proper to thought, and not just one of the attributes that would be assumed by an invariable positing of being. Modal thought—intelligence opposed to reason which posits and articulates the seamless coherence of being—is philosophy. Philosophy, a modality of negation (but negativity never negative enough—never to the point of not being connected with being, of not having anything to do with it), is the thought of Plato, Aristotle, Descartes, Spinoza, Kant, Hegel and Bergson. Philosophy is also their thought such as we disciples reflect on its modalities, such as it is renewed in us, as if it had no history. "And not until you have all denied me will I return among you," says Zarathustra. It is obvious that, to Madame Delhomme, Nietzsche also belongs to the high society we have just enumerated.

But the interruption[4] of history by philosophy is brought about in the relationship between philosophy and the philosopher. This relationship is conceived by Jeanne Delhomme in terms of concepts, not of consciousness. Philosophy is not the individuation of philosophy understood as consciousness engendering, within time, thoughts that think the world and itself. As soon as consciousness claims an originary role, history, continuity and ontology return. Rather than the *of* of the "consciousness of something," in which the genitive turns into a genesis, Madame Delhomme prefers the *of* of the "concept of something," but without this *of* being taken as designating an objective relation, since it is precisely the priority of the objective that modal thought challenges. The philosopher, as idea of the idea, is the particularization of philosophy, tearing the latter free from the history of ideas (into which it can always be integrated, by eliminating its particularity). The incessant return of philosophy to the philosopher is the very discontinuity of the history of ideas, negativity (never sufficiently negative) freeing itself from the possibility of theses. It does not suffice to be an *I* to interrupt history!

This is an extreme Bergsonism, at odds with Bergsonism, and a curious convergence with the whole current antisubjectivism, with an entire epiphenomenology of the *I*, in which the uniqueness of the *I* is inseparable from intelligence and language. But in that separation between particularity and psychism, it is possible to find new terms in which to pose the problem of the *I*; it does not suffice to say that it is the source or center of psychic acts. There is, moreover, in this particularization of philosophies, an answer to the problem by their multiplicity, which has arisen since it has become clear that the synthesis of all the philosophies is but another philosophy. The scandal of multiplicity would, in this view, be necessary to philosophy, which is modal thought, the sole way of escaping history. We have not, then, come to the end of philosophy, which is the pre-eminently spiritual act, since it is on one side and everything else is on the other. It does not even succeed in finding a place for itself in culture.

Whence the idea of a spontaneity without a trace—with no going back—that nothing burdens down. To walk forward without having to look back on the road traveled, without having to go back, to expend one's energies without keeping track and without having to give an account, without all those weighty matters that make for a settled way of life—is this the inattentiveness [*inconscience*] of the living, or, beyond all attentiveness [*conscience*], the extreme intelligence of the *beyond being*? Does lucidity not culminate in a wonder that can no longer be thought reflectively, and that consequently transcends the concern over foundation? Philosophy would be that spontaneity,

> an absolute event that does not take its place or rank in any succession; a rupture, not a filiation, an instant with neither past nor future. It imposes and posits itself without references or antecedent. It enters into no process, and does not constitute the moment—not even the privileged moment—of a progressive, growing evolution, because it is an original concept and a new language. History without materiality, succession without trace, such is the history of the philosophies. Appearance without representation; advent without postulation of reality, present without past—such is a philosophy."[5]

Philosophy, considered as modal thought, separates itself so radically from being that it does not return to it even by way of thinking the conditions of its own possibility. It is true that certain expressions, such as that being itself is "a concept drawn from nothing," or "the word is not sustained by the real, but sustains it," are astonishing in a book that breaks free (and that is surely one of its novelties) from transcendental philosophy. But the overall intent is to be free from the conditions of being as well as from being itself. Indirect dependence upon the transcendental possible is as oppressive to this philosophy as is dogmatism. It is a philosophy that leaves being and history—the order of the day—all their triumphs. It opposes to them only the negativity of an interruption, of a night more lucid than day, of an extra-vagence of the intelligence that Plato may have had in mind in speaking of delirium in the *Phaedrus*. Or perhaps the interstice in which all is possible, where "all is permitted to thought and where nothing is true,"[6] is the interworld inhabited by the gods of Epicurus. It is an artificial eternity that brings to mind the one that, in *Man's Fate* by Malraux (to whom the author of *La pensée et le réel* previously devoted a book),[7] is ever parallel to the Revolution in its confrontation with the Real. Here, the "narcotic" is the intelligence, escape is toward meaning

note ref. to Blanchot

outside being, the absolute is thought in terms other than being, and it would not be valid, in this view, to argue against this escape by pointing out the finitude of the transcendental conditions of the very thought that leaves those conditions behind. The negativity of thought that becomes language is never sufficiently negative, and breaks through the wall of its finitude.

And indeed, here, this "is never sufficiently" is ambiguous, and might indicate the breakthrough as well as to the impossibility of interruption. We are reminded of Blanchot's work, in which the infinite of negativity is the incessant return of the *there is* at the heart of all disappearance, and in which poetic language, the essence of language, is but the disturbance caused by this return. The "nothing" on which intelligence focuses in order to draw being from it—does this "nothing" not already carry a reference to being? Can a distinction be made between poetic language and the privileged language of the philosopher? Based on what criterion? If modal thought can free itself from the thetic language that envelops it and that is capable of relating the very ruptures of thought, can it silence the murmur of the *there is*? Nothing is said in *La pensée et le réel* on the difference between the philosopher's language and language *tout court*, as if to indicate that the secret of language might begin with "Pass me the bread", "After you, sir!", "Give me fifty cents' worth of ice-cream", or "What a nice day!".

The notion of modal thought, which, in the order of knowledge, adumbrates the divorce between expression and its object that is called pure poetry or pure painting in the order of the beautiful—that notion, which is at bottom the search for musicality, in which knowledge goes back to a vibration of the intelligence, to the infinite negativity of its modulation, in which it becomes an adverb called modality—that thought leads us to something that might be called non-figurative philosophy. But modal thought is not just the reflection of an extreme refinement in the Western form of expression. It daringly undertakes to cease thinking in terms of things and objects. Modern philosophy, in various forms, from Hegel to Bergson, substituting becoming and duration for substance, has tended toward that de-objectification or de-reification of thought that perhaps requires a de-ontologization, as Plato's *Parmenides* had fleetingly glimpsed. Husserl's phenomenology seemed, to Heidegger and Scheler, to promise such a thing with the notion of intentionality. It is true that in Husserl the objectifying belief is in abeyance, slumbering beneath the practical and axiological modalities of the intention. But do the emotive access to values and the non-intellectual comprehension of the being of beings obliterate the intent, however formal, of objectification? Being returns in intentionality's durable threads, in which history is already being woven. Thought, appearing not as a *thesis*, but as a *manner*, while not dominating history, interrupts it. The freedom of escape! But are the real travelers indeed those who, as Baudelaire says, leave for the sake of leaving?[8]

The departure from being, leaving behind the serious and reasonable balance of assets and liabilities, the giving up of freedoms devoid of excess or deficit and involving limited responsibilities, the refusal of history's rigorous accounting in favor of an interval [*entre-temps*] of gratuitousness: is this not deeply ambiguous or enigmatic—enigmatic with an enigma that confers upon Jeanne Delhomme's project a significance transcending its own choice? Is not the modality of her thought situated between the freedom of escape, of play, freedom without responsibilities (which Eugen Fink, in a recent work,[9] views as being among the conditions of the world), on one hand, and on the other the gratuitousness of sacrifice in the guise of non-freedom, responsibility as unreasonable as the irresponsibility of play, vocation of the creature answering beyond his initiatives, i.e. answering *for the others*, and, by that very fact, placing himself outside or beyond being? Should not the relation to *others* be expressed in *terms* different from the *negativity* of *otherness*? A relation in which the servitudes and encumbrances of history appear in a new modality, that of ethics transcending ontology. History as the ultimate figuration of thought not only signifies thought's subordination to the dogmas that command the thinker without revealing themselves to him: it is the reversal, by the historical narrative, of every rupture of history into the history of a rupture. The notion of a modal thought whose negativity tears the durable threads of intentionality strikes a blow at the reversible genitive by which all transcendence of being turns into the being of that transcendence, in which nothing is wonderful enough to prevent the spell of exteriority from being broken and changed into the history of a spell.

Perhaps as opposed to what the book we have just read says *thetically*, there is in it the freeing-up of an ambiguous modality of beyond being. It is as if, behind being [*l'être*], one could hear the sarcastic laughter of irresponsibility, for which the freedom within being is not free enough; but beyond being [*l'essence*] there would extend the goodness of unbounded responsibility, for which that freedom is not generous enough.

6 Jacques Derrida: Wholly Otherwise

1 Today Is Tomorrow

Does Derrida's work constitute a line of demarcation running through the development of Western thought in a manner analogous to Kantianism, which separated dogmatic from critical philosophy? Are we once again at the end of a naivety, an unsuspected dogmatism that slumbered in the depths of what we took to be the critical spirit? We may well ask ourselves that question. The Idea, as the end of a series that begins in intuition but is unable to reach its end within it—the Idea "in the Kantian sense of the term" as it is called[1]—is, according to Derrida, operative at the heart of intuition itself. A transcendental semblance, engendering a metaphysics, produces an illusion at the heart of presence itself, which is incessantly lacking to itself. Is this a new break in the history of philosophy? It would also show its continuity. The history of philosophy is probably nothing but a growing awareness of the difficulty of thinking.

In the meantime, we tread a *no-man's land*,[2] an in-between that is uncertain even of the uncertainties that flicker everywhere. Suspension of truths! Unusual times! We all feel this as we write, perhaps to the degree that we catch ourselves using familiar ideas with excessive caution, while the new critique would question both the sense of risk and the virtue of prudence. We become aware of a new style of thought as we read these exceptionally precise, yet very strange texts. In *Speech and Phenomena*, which overthrows logocentric discourse, there is not a haphazard phrase. A marvelous rigor, learned at the school of phenomenology, by devoting extreme attention to Husserl's discrete moves and Heidegger's more sweeping ones, but applied with consistency and consummate skill: an inversion of the limiting concept into precondition, of defect into source, of abyss into condition, of discourse into locus [*lieu*], and the inversion of these very inversions into destiny: the concepts having been stripped of their ontic resonance, freed from the alternative of true or false. At the outset, everything is in place; after a few pages or paragraphs of formidable calling into question, nothing is left inhabitable for thought. This is, all philosophical significance aside, a purely literary effect, a new *frisson*, Derrida's poetry. In reading him, I always see the 1940 exodus again. The retreating military unit reaches an area that still doesn't know what is happening. The cafés are open, the ladies are at the "Ladies' Latest" stores, barbers are cutting hair, bakers are baking, viscounts meeting and telling one another viscount stories. An hour later, everything is torn down [*déconstruit*] and left desolate: the houses closed up, or abandoned with their doors open, are emptied of their inhabitants, who are caught up in a stream of cars and pedestrians through the streets, which have reverted to their "deep past" ["*profond jadis*"][3] of routes, traced out in an immemorial past by the great migrations. In those days of a time between times, there occurred the following symbolic episode. Somewhere between Paris and Alençon, a half-drunk barber invited the soldiers who were passing by on the road (the "boys," [les "*petits gars*"] as he called them, in a patriotic language gliding above the waters, or keeping afloat in the chaos) to come into his little shop for a free shave. He, along with his two co-workers, shaved them for free and suddenly it was today. The essential procrastination—the future *différence*—was reabsorbed into the present. Time was reaching its end with the end, or the interim, of France. Or was the barber as delirious as the fourth form of

[margin handwritten notes: "the effect of Derrida's 'poetry' = the sudden flight of refugees"]

delirium in the *Phaedrus,* a delirium in which, since Plato, the discourse of Western metaphysics is conducted?[4]

2 The Pass-Time

Philosophy as defeat, desertion of an impossible presence. Western metaphysics, and probably our entire history in Europe, may turn out to have been, through a conceptual apparatus that Derrida dismantles or deconstructs, the edification and preservation of that presence: the founding of the very idea of foundation, the founding of all the relations that become experience, i.e. the manifestation of beings architectonically arranged on a basis that supports them, the manifestation of a world that is capable of being constructed, or, as the expression goes, of constituting itself for a transcendental apperception. Presence of the present, gathering, synchrony. Leave nothing lying about! Don't lose anything! Keep everything that is yours! The security of the peoples of Europe behind their borders and the walls of their houses, assured of their property (*Eigenheit* that becomes *Eigentum*),[5] is not the sociological condition of metaphysical thought, but the very project of such thought. A project impossible of accomplishment, ever deferred, a *messianic future* as that missing present. *Speech and Phenomena* denounces this metaphysical simulacrum of presence, which is sustained by the voice that listens to itself: presence and possession united in self-consciousness. A simulacrum or an illusion, but prior to ontic illusion and appearance, prior to the distinction between reality and fantasy. All materialism is marked by this, as is all idealism.

The desertion of presence, carried out to the point of desertion of the true, to the point of meanings that are no longer held to respond to the summons of Knowledge. Truth is no longer at the level of eternal or omnitemporal truth—but this is a relativism beyond historicism's wildest dreams. An exile or casting adrift of Knowledge beyond skepticism, which remained enamored of truth, even if it did not feel itself capable of embracing it. Henceforth meanings do not converge on truth. Truth is not the main thing! Being does not succeed in being all the way: its bankrupt way of life needs more time to pay, recourse to signs, amidst a presence that eludes itself; but in the signified of these signs nothing but signs are produced. Husserl's notion of infinite iteration, which he understood by means of the "idea in the Kantian sense," endlessly postpones the contemporaneousness of the signified with a presence. The latter, always pointed toward, escapes prehension. Hence the wearing away of the signified, releasing a system of signs, of signifiers without signifieds, of a language that no full meaning guides. Thus is expressed, in the guise of dissemination, the *différence* in which presence is deconstructed, a postponement without due date to be met, which time is, or, more precisely, which the pass-time itself is. Play within the interstices of being, in which the centers of gravity are not the same as in the world. But are there centers? Is there gravity? Is there there is [*Y a-t-il*]? All is otherwise, if one can still speak of being.

What remains constructed after deconstruction is, to be sure, the stern architecture of the discourse that deconstructs and uses the verb "to be" in the present tense in predicative statements. A discourse in the course of which, amidst the quaking of truth's underpinnings and in opposition to the self-evidence of the lived presence, which seems to offer presence a last refuge, Derrida still has the strength to utter: "Is this certain?"[6] As if anything could be certain at that point, and as if certainty or uncertainty should still matter.

One might be tempted to draw an argument from this recourse to logocentric language in opposing that very language, in order to question the validity of the deconstruction thus produced. That is a course that has frequently been followed in refuting skepticism; but the latter, thrown to the ground and trampled on at first, would right itself and return as philosophy's legitimate child. It is a course Derrida himself, perhaps, has not always disdained to follow in his polemics.

But in pursuing that course, we would risk missing the significance of that very inconsistency. We would miss the

the non-simultaneity of Saying & the law of contradiction
the Said and suspends of non-

incompressible non-simultaneity of the Said and the Saying, the discrepancy in their correlation: a very slight discrepancy, but wide enough for the discourse of skepticism to creep into it without being choked off by the contradiction between what its *said* means and the meaning of the very fact of uttering a *said*. It is as if the two meanings lacked the simultaneity that would be required for contradiction to sunder their connection. It is as if the correlation of the *Saying* and the *Said* were a diachrony of the unassemblable; and as if the situation of the Saying were already, for the Said, a "retention memory," but without the lapse of the instants of the Saying letting themselves be recovered in this memory.

The truth of truths, then, cannot be gathered into an instant, nor into a synthesis in which the so-called movement of the dialectic would stop. It [the truth of truths] is in the Said and the Un-Said [*le Dédit*] and the Said Otherwise—return, reiteration, reduction: the history of philosophy, or its preliminary. Is that what Blanchot suggests in *L'attente L'oubli,* giving the subject of the statement a predicate that is successively in the affirmative and the negative?[7] The truth of truths may not have the style of verbal dissemination; but it is of the same non-world, the end of the "eternal truths," whose death-throes and figures of convulsion are unsuspected by both empiricism and historical relativism. It is therefore not absurd that a rigorous reflection should vouchsafe us a glimpse of these interstices of being, in which that very reflection unsays itself. Nothing can be seen without thematization, or without the oblique rays reflected by it, even in the case of the non-thematizable.

The path leading toward these pathless "places," the subsoil of our empirical places, does not, in any case, open out upon the dizziness caused by those who—frightfully well informed and prodigiously intelligent and more Derridian than Derrida—interpret the latter's extraordinary work with the help of all the key words at once, though neither having, nor leaving to their readers, the time to return to the thinking that was contemporary with those words.

3 The Chiasmus

Derrida's critique—which frees time from its subordination to the present, which no longer takes the past and the future as modes, modifications, or modulations of presence, which arrests a thinking that reasons upon signs as if upon signifieds—thinks through to the end Bergson's critique of being and Kant's critique of metaphysics. Through that deconstruction of presence, the testimony of consciousness to itself loses its Cartesian privilege. Must we excuse ourselves for quoting these old authors? It doesn't prevent this doggedly rectilinear thinking [*"jusqu'au boutisme"*] from leading us into the strange non-order of the excluded middle, in which the disjunction of the yes and no, the imperious alternative, thanks to which computers decide about the universe, is challenged.

It will be less readily recognized—Derrida would probably refuse to do so—that this critique of being in its eternal presence of ideality allows us, for the first time in the history of the West, to conceive of *the being of the creature* without resorting to the ontic narrative of a divine operation—without treating the "being" [*"être"*] of the creature as *a* being [*un étant*] from the outset, without bringing to bear negative and empirical concepts, such as contingency or "generation and corruption"—concepts as ontic as the incorruptibility of the Whole. For the first time, the "less being," which is that of the creature, is shown in its verbality of verb. It is true that, in order to avoid the return of the metaphysics of presence in that thought, Derrida would have the reader seek, for the operative concept of the sign of a failed presence, a reference other than the failure of that presence, and a place [*lieu*] other than the Said of language (oral or written)—a place other than a language, which, completely at the disposal of the speaker, itself feigns synchrony, the preeminent presence of a system of signs that is already presupposed by any empirical simultaneity. But would not any attempt to express this lack of presence positively be still one more way of returning to presence, with which positivity converges? To say that this lack is still being is to turn in the circle of being and nothingness (which are ultimate concepts, but of the same degree) and retain nothing of being but a taste for unhappiness. It is no doubt surer than the hoped-for happiness, which, beyond the pleasures and intoxications, is the impossible fullness of presence. But is there no way out of ontology?

The fact that language is grafted upon time's most invisible difference, that its saying is dislocated from its said, and that the correlation is not rigorous (already rupturing the unity of apperception, and, consequently, the possibilities of experience)—certainly sets language apart from everything empirical, which is exhausted in presence and lack of presence. Indeed, it would be necessary one day to find, setting out from Saying and its own meaning, Saying's correlation with the Said—and this is not impossible. But the Saying is not exhausted in this *Said*, and the sign did not spring from the soil of the ontology of the Said, to receive from it its paradoxical structure of relation (which astonished Plato to the point of pushing him to parricide)[8] and make up for a self-eluding presence. The sign, like the Saying, is the extra-ordinary event (running counter to presence) of exposure to others, of subjection to others; i.e. the event of subjectivity. It is the one-for-the-other. It is meaning that is not exhausted in a simple absence of intuition and of presence.[9] I enquire: Whence the sign from which the presence that is lacking to itself is made, or the inassemblable diachrony from which creatureliness is made? It does not begin (if it does begin, if it is not anarchy through and through) as a Said. Is not substitution, replacement, the one-for-the-other—in its decisive suspension of the *for itself*— the for-the-other of my responsibility for others? The difference between the Same and the Other is the non-indifference for the other of fraternity. What appears truly in deconstructive analysis as a lacking to self is not *the surplus* (which would be yet another promise of happiness and a residuum of ontology) but the *better* of proximity, an excellence, an elevation, the ethics of before being or the Good beyond Being, again to quote an ancient author. The presence of the present that Descartes discovered in the *cogito*, without suspecting the unconscious that undermined it, immediately burst apart with the idea of God that it could not contain.

I shall not prolong the trajectory of a thought in the opposite direction from the one toward which its verb disseminates itself. The ridiculous ambition[10] of "improving" a true philosopher is assuredly not my intent. Our crossing of paths is already very good, and it is probably the very modality of the philosophical encounter. In emphasizing the primordial importance of the questions raised by Derrida, I have desired to express the pleasure of a contact at the heart of a chiasmus.

7 Edmond Jabès Today

A response to two questions asked by Les Nouveaux Cahiers.
1. In today's literary scene, what place do you assign to the work of Edmond Jabès?

2. How, specifically, do you define Jabès's work (but without limiting its scope) with respect to its relation to exile, to wandering, and consequently to the condition of being Jewish, which the author identifies with that of writing and being a writer?

Question 1

Is it certain that a true poet occupies a place? Is he not that which, in the eminent sense of the term, *loses its place*, ceases occupation, precisely, and is thus the very opening of space, neither the transparency nor the emptiness of which (no more than night, nor the volume of beings) yet displays the bottomlessness or the excellence, the heaven that in it is possible, its "heavenhood" or its "celestiality," if one may use such neologisms? Bottomlessness or height ("the highest abyss," according to Jabès) into which all interiority sinks, splitting open, in the air more external than exteriority, to the core; as if simple human breathing were but a gasping, as if poetic saying rose above that breathlessness to reach at last deep respiration, inspiration which is the de-claustration of all things, the de-nucleation of being—

or its transcendence—from which nothing more is missing but one's fellow man. "I am nothing but the spoken word," says Jabès. "I need a face."

The fact that that opening occurs in the clauses of Jabès that retain their syntactic decency and as it were uncork the words, not in order that they may give off some secret meaning, but rather that, undergoing fission, they may be broken up into their sense and letters and give off the non-place of an absolutely unprotected space, a kind of intra-nuclear space devoid of images, without mirages or prestige or imaginary foyers of extension for a dioptrics, but a field besieged by God—that is what would prompt me to say that Jabès's work occupies no place. And, for my part, when I have his texts before me I forget that his writing has writing as its theme (if indeed the security of a theme can still be held as a guarantee for anything at all in writing such as this); I forget that Jabès has his part in the world and trends of modern letters.

Question 2

That opening of space—opening in the superlative—produced in the guise of an inspired subjectivity (inspired to the point of uttering its saying as a quotation: either in quotation marks, or preceded or interrupted by a "he used to say," or a "said he") makes the word God suddenly appear, understood as the word, "eye" ["*oeil*"] or written as "of eyes" ["d'*yeux*"].[1] "Do you know," he says, "that the final period in the book is an eye, that it is lidless?" This is not, in that opening, a resorting to an obscure old word of right-thinking people, but a pronunciation—from before any rememberable beginning—in which God is heard. Declaustration as delivery to a lidless Eye, but in the "Desire of being seen," in which the word Law [*Loi*] imposes itself upon Jabès: exposure, without defense, to an attention the hyperbole of which is exigency; is that not what the "sleepless" attention of the "guardian of Israel" is? That is, in any case, the Jewish moment of Jabès's work; I mean its human moment.

Need I quote Psalm 139, summarized in the Talmud by the strange symbol of Adam created with two faces: with one head—all face—without any background, any shadow for secret thoughts or mental reservations, without any possible break with this God, even by the choice of Evil?

A Judaism of wandering, of exile, in Jabès? The exegesis of some point or other of Jewish tradition that had come down to him? There is that element. Those are themes. They are the joy of minor poets. In Jabès, they are still turning in the vertigo that comes from what he calls "the vertiginous place of the book."

8 Kierkegaard: Existence and Ethics

1 Truth Triumphant

The strong notion of existence which European thought owes to Kierkegaard amounts to maintaining human subjectivity—and the dimension of interiority it opens—as absolute, separated, standing on the hither side of objective Being; but it also involves, paradoxically, defending the irreducible position of the subject against idealism, which had nonetheless given it philosophical status, on the basis of a pre-philosophical experience. For idealism was going so far as either to reduce man to a disembodied and impassible point, and his interiority to the eternity of a logical act, or, with Hegel, to letting the human subject be absorbed by the Being that this subject uncovered. Idealism claimed that the unfolding of Being by thought allowed the subject to rise above itself and hand over its last secrets to Reason. It was as if a painter, upon completing his work, were to find himself caught up in the very painting beneath his brush, and transported to a world of his own creation.

Kierkegaard opposed that claim by denying that the movement in which idealism grasped subjectivity was originally thinking, that is, he denied that it was that power of "taking as theme" which totalizes experiences, shows them to be comparable, and consequently generalizable, forming System and

Idea through their differences and oppositions. He denied that subjectivity came down to that power that simultaneously places all being on a par with the thinker and expresses the thinker in the beings he or she fashions in thinking. Thus, he denied that Being was the correlate of thought.

In what, then, does the subjectivity of the subject reside? Kierkegaard could not resort to the particularity of feeling and enjoyment, as opposed to the generosity of the concept. The stage he called esthetic, and which is that of sensible dispersion, leads to the impasse of despair in which subjectivity loses itself. But at the stage representing the other term of the alternative, the ethical stage (a stage at which the inner life is translated in terms of legal order, carried out in society, in loyalty to institutions and principles and in communication with mankind), totalizing, generalizing thought is incapable of containing the thinker. Exteriority cannot match human interiority. The subject has a secret, for ever inexpressible, which determines his or her very subjectivity. A secret that is not simply knowledge about which one refrains from speaking, but one that, identified especially with the burn of sin, remains of itself inexpressible. No truth triumphant, i.e. rational or universal, no expression could express or assuage it.

But that incommunicable burn, that "thorn in the side," attests to subjectivity as a *tensing on oneself* [*tension sur soi*] in which there can be recognized, beyond the philosophical notion of subjectivity, the return to the Christian experience, and even to its pagan sources: existence tensed over itself, open to the outside in an attitude of impatience and of waiting—an impatience that the outer world (of people and things), wrapped in a relaxed, impassive thought, cannot satisfy. And beyond that thirst for salvation, there is an older tension of the human soul (perhaps for this reason "naturally" Christian) that consumes itself with desires.

The subjectivity deriving from that early experience, common to both the philosophy of existence and speculative philosophy, is a way for a being to make its appearance [*se produire*], a way such that its identification is not a simple logical tautology that would *say* it is part of being—the repetition of A is A—and that would be indifferent to its way of gliding above nothingness, or its *meteoric* aspect [*météorie*]. The tautology activates, in a sense, that emergence from nothingness and that forward surge. Before all language, the identification of subjectivity is the fact of being's attachment to its being. The identification of A as A is the anxiety of A for A. The subjectivity of the subject is an identification of the Same in its care for the Same. It is egotism. Subjectivity is a *Me*.

The thought that Hegel's idealism put into subjectivity also had that egocentric orientation of the subject as its point of departure. The dialectic's remarkable effort consisted in showing the necessity of the conversion of that egotism into Being and Truth, and, in so doing, in revealing a thinking that lay dormant in the subjectivity of the subject. At a certain moment the tension upon itself relaxes to become consciousness of self, the *I* grasps itself in a totality, under a general law, on the basis of a truth that triumphs—that is, that leads to discourse. Which is, in fact, the passing of subjectivity into philosophy.

But to discern in that discourse—in that *possibility of speaking*, attained as a prolongation of totalizing thought—a distant *impossibility* of discourse, the shadow of evening in the midday sun ... to sense—through that philosophy of totality that relaxes subjective egotism (though it be sublime as the thirst for salvation)—the end of philosophy, ending in a political totalitarianism in which human beings are no longer the source of their language, but reflections of the impersonal logos, or roles played by figures: all this constitutes the value of the Kierkegaardian notion of existence and its deeply Protestant protest against systems. But, we might ask ourselves whether the return to a subjectivity that turns away from thought, i.e. that refuses ever-triumphant truth, the thought suspected of lying and *distraction* when it claims to calm our anxieties, does not lead us to other forms of violence. We must ask ourselves whether the subjectivity that is irreducible to objective being could not be understood in virtue of a different principle than its egotism, and whether the true ethical stage is correctly described by Kierkegaard as generality and equivalence of the inner and the outer. Might not existence be posited outside of both speculative totalitarianism and Kierkegaardian non-philosophy?

2 Truth Persecuted

To truth triumphant—accessible to the knowledge in which existence would have the illusion (but only the illusion) of "unraveling itself"—Kierkegaard opposes belief that is authentic because reflective of the incomparable status of subjectivity. Belief is not an imperfect knowledge of a truth that would be, in itself, perfect and triumphant, imposing its sway from the start upon everyone's thinking—the knowledge of a truth that is merely uncertain. For in that case belief would be a mere degradation of knowledge; the subjectivity sustaining it would be mistakenly viewed as an opaque area running through the sunlit field of exteriority before fading away.

Belief translates the condition of an existence that no "outside" could contain, and that is at the same time needy and indigent, poor with that radical poverty, that irremediable poverty, that absolute hunger that is, in the final analysis, what sin is. *Belief is linked to a truth that suffers.* The truth that *suffers* and is persecuted is very different from a truth improperly approached. It is so different that in Kierkegaard's eyes it is through suffering truth that one can describe the very manifestation of the divine: simultaneity of All and Nothingness, Relation to a Person both present and absent—to a humiliated God who suffers, dies and leaves those whom he saves in despair. A certainty that coexists with an absolute uncertainty—to the point that one may wonder whether that Revelation itself is not contrary to the essence of that crucified truth, whether God's suffering and the lack of recognition of the truth would not reach their highest degree in a total *incognito.*

The contradiction between presence and absence, in which belief maintains itself, remains unreconciled—like an open wound, in a state of endless bleeding. The refusal of the synthesis is not in this case an intellectual weakness. It is precisely in keeping with this new mode of truth. Suffering and humiliation are not the result of a mishap that befalls truth from without: they are inscribed in its essence of truth and, in a sense, in its divinity itself. Thus faith, the going forth from self, the only possible going forth for subjectivity, is the solitary tête-à-tête with what for Kierkegaard admits of nothing but the tête-à-tête: God. The *salto-mortale* executed by existence to pass from absence to presence is ever to be resumed. Possession is never certain. If the synthesis were to be realized, the tête-à-tête would be broken off. It could then *be said*. Subjectivity would lose its tension upon itself, its contraction, its underlying egotism; it would enter exteriority and generality. It would become philosophy, or the future life. In belief, existence seeks recognition, as does consciousness in Hegel. It struggles for that recognition by begging for forgiveness and salvation. But that recognition is granted by a truth that is itself held up to ridicule, not recognized and ever *to be recognized*, and the subjectivism of subjectivity is never completed.

But the idea of a truth that suffers transforms all seeking after truth—all relation to exteriority—into an inner drama. In the eyes of the outer world it is indiscretion, scandal. Its discourse directed to the outer world is anger and invective. It is ruthless. The truth that suffers does not open man to other men but to God, in solitude. That existence, the interiority of which is too big for the outer world, and cannot enter it, is thus, in the eyes of many, in the violence of the modern world and its cult of Ardor and Passion. It carries within it an irresponsibility, a ferment of disintegration. Accursed or cursing philosophers suddenly emerge, like accursed poets.[1] But we might ask ourselves whether the exaltation of pure faith, the correlate of truth crucified (the "phenomenology" which no one has developed with greater rigor than Kierkegaard), is not itself the ultimate consequence of that still natural tension of being on itself that I have alluded to above as egotism. Egotism is not an ugly vice of the subject's, but its ontology, as we find in the sixth proposition of Part III of Spinoza's *Ethics*: "Every being makes every effort insofar as it is in it to persevere in its being"; and in Heidegger's expression about existence existing in such a way that its Being has this very Being as an issue.[2]

Kierkegaard's philosophy has marked contemporary thought so deeply that the reservations and even the rejections it may elicit are yet forms of that influence. The seductiveness of the later Heidegger is due in part to the rigorously ontological style of his thought of Being. That thought opposes Kierkegaard's subjectivism with such force only because it has pursued the adventure of existence to the end, and may have contributed most in *Being and Time* to raising to the level of philosophical categories the notions that, ':. Kierkegaard, still retain the meaning of subjective metamorphoses.[3] Similarly, the return of Hegelian thought and the fascination it holds are not solely attributable to the foundation it provides for the great political questions of today, which preoccupy both the proponents and the adversaries of Marxism, that is, the entire thinking world of this mid-twentieth century. Neo-Hegelianism derives a kind of nobility from its reaction against the exacerbated subjectivism of existence. After one hundred years of Kierkegaardian protest, one would like to get beyond that pathos. The idle distraction that Kierkegaard, borrowing Pascal's notion of vain recreation [*divertissement*] denounces in the systems, has gradually been replaced by an obvious immodesty.

We may ask ourselves whether, in a sense, a part of that authenticity Kierkegaard has made appealing to us does not consist in the forgetting and sublimating of that same tension on oneself that still defines Kierkegaardian subjectivity; and whether a renunciation of self should not accompany that desire for salvation so underrated by systematic philosophy.

In the dialogue between Anima and Animus, between the individual, sensitive soul and Universal Spirit, the Spirit's voice seems to me, even in its Hegelian form, to limit the indulgence that the Soul and its interiority always have toward themselves.

Recourse to the Being of beings that reveals itself and elicits human subjectivity only in its truth and its mystery, recourse to the impersonal structures of Spirit beyond the arbitrary and imagination: both take on the virile and ruthless accents to which those coming out of the existentialist experience may be sensitive, not just as one is sensitive to a change of climate, but as one likes that with which one is familiar. Kierkegaard's thought has contributed to this, by its intransigent vehemence, by its taste for scandal. There is henceforth, in any case, a new tone in philosophy, which Nietzsche took up when he began to philosophize "with the blows of a hammer."

Harshness and aggressivity in thought, which until then characterized the least scrupulous and most realist action, henceforth justify this violence and terrorism. It is not just a question of literary form. Violence emerges in Kierkegaard at the precise moment when, moving beyond the esthetic stage, existence can no longer limit itself to what it takes to be an ethical stage and enters the religious one, the domain of belief. This latter is no longer justified in the outer world. Even within, it is at once communication and solitude, and hence violence and passion. Thus begins the disdain for the ethical basis of being, the somehow secondary nature of all ethical phenomena that, through Nietzsche, has led us to the amoralism of the most recent philosophers.

3 Diacony[4]

The entire polemics between Kierkegaard and speculative philosophy presupposes subjectivity as tensed on itself, existence as a care that a being takes for its own existence, as a torment for self. The ethical means the general to Kierkegaard. The singularity of the *I* would be lost under the rule that is valid for all. Generality can neither contain nor express the secret of the *I*, infinitely needy and distressed for itself.

Is the relation to the Other that entering into, and disappearing within, generality? *That is what must be asked in opposition to Kierkegaard as well as in opposition to Hegel.* If the relation to exteriority cannot form a totality whose parts can be compared and generalized, it is not because the *I* keeps its secret within the system, but because the exteriority in which human beings show us their faces shatters the totality.[5] That shattering of the system because of the Other [*Autrui*] is not an apocalyptic image, but the very impossibility, for a thinking that reduces all otherness to the same, of reducing the Other. An impossibility that does not remain in its negative meaning, but immediately puts the *I* in question. This putting in question signifies the responsibility of the *I* for the Other. Subjectivity *is* in that responsibility and only irreducible subjectivity can assume a responsibility. That is what constitutes the ethical.

To be myself means, then, to be unable to escape responsibility. This excess of being, this existential exaggeration called *being me*—this outcrop of *ipseity* in being, is accomplished as a swelling of responsibility. The putting in question of the *I* in the face of the Other is a new tension in the *I*, a tension that is not a tensing on oneself. Instead of destroying the *I*, the putting in question binds it to the Other in an incomparable, unique manner. Not bound in the way matter is bound to the mass of which it is a part, nor as an organ to the organism in which it has its function. These sorts of bonds, which are mechanical and organic, would dissolve the *I* into a totality.

The *I* is bound to the *not-I*, as if the entire fate of the Other [l'Autre] were in our hands. The uniqueness of the *I* consists in the fact that no one can answer in his or her place. The putting in question of the *I* by the Other is not initially a reflective act in which the *I* reappears, and is gloriously and serenely surveyed from on high, but neither is it the entry of the *I* into a supra-personal, coherent, universal discourse. The putting in question of the *I* by the Other is, *ipso facto*, an election, the promotion to a privileged place on which all that is not me depends.

This election signifies the most radical commitment there is, total altruism. The responsibility that rids the *I* of its im-perialism and egotism (be it the egotism of salvation) does not transform it into a moment of the universal order: it confirms it in its ipseity, in its central place in being, the support of the universe.

The *I* before the Other is infinitely responsible. The Other is the poor, the destitute, and nothing about that Stranger can be indifferent to it. It reaches the apogee of its existence as an *I* when everything in the Other concerns it. The fullness of power in which the sovereignty of the *I* maintains itself extends to the Other not in order to conquer it, but to support it. But at the same time, to support the burden of the Other is to confirm it in its substantiality, to situate it above the *I*. The *I* remains accountable for that burden to the same one whom it supports. The one *to* whom I am answerable is the same one *for* whom I am answerable. The "for whom" and the "to whom" coincide. It is this double movement of responsibility that designates the dimension of height. It forbids me to exercise that responsibility as pity, for I must give my account to the same person for whom I am accountable. It forbids my exercising that responsibility as an unconditional obedience within a hierarchic order, for I am responsible for the very one who commands me.

Kierkegaard has a predilection for the biblical story of the sacrificing of Isaac.[6] Thus, he describes the encounter with God as a subjectivity rising to the religious level: God above the ethical order! His interpretation of this story can doubtless be given a different orientation. Perhaps Abraham's ear for hearing the voice that brought him back to the ethical order was the highest moment in this drama. And Kierkegaard never speaks of the situation in which Abraham enters into dialogue with God to intercede in favor of Sodom and Gomorrah, in the name of the just who may be present there.[7] In that passage, Abraham is fully aware of his nothingness and mortality. "I am but dust and ashes" practically opens the dialogue, and the annihilating flame of divine ire burns before Abraham's eyes each time he intervenes. But death is powerless, for life receives meaning from an infinite responsibility, a fundamental *diacony* that constitutes the subjectivity of the subject—without that responsibility, completely tendered toward the Other, leaving any leisure for a return to self.

9 A Propos of "Kierkegaard vivant"

Among the contributions devoted to Kierkegaard on the occasion of that philosopher's centenary (celebrated in Paris in 1964), which were published in 1966 by Gallimard as *Kierkegaard vivant*,[1] two of my interventions were included (pp. 232–234 and 286–288), but in a form that distorted them. This was attributed to the probably defective recording of a spoken text.

The publisher, to whom immediately after the publication of *Kierkegaard vivant* I offered a reworked text, written with extreme care (in order to respect the pagination of the first edition), amiably promised to use it in eventual later editions in place of the pages on which I had pointed out the defects. It has no doubt been impossible for him to do so to date [1966].

The publication in French of my article on Kierkegaard,[2] which appeared in German in May, 1963, in the Zurich journal *Schweizer Monatshefte*, offers a long-awaited opportunity for me to restore the meaning—though in a different context—to reflections that in *Kierkegaard vivant* are honored by the proximity of illustrious names.

My first intervention is in connection with the remark by Jean Hyppolite (p. 218) on the annoyance one may feel with Kierkegaard.

My second intervention is occasioned by a reflection by Gabriel Marcel (p. 285) on the extreme inner rending in Kierkegaard.

I

What disturbs me in Kierkegaard may be reduced to two points.

The first point. Kierkegaard rehabilitated subjectivity—the unique, the singular—with incomparable strength. But in protesting against the absorption of subjectivity by Hegel's universality, he bequeathed to the history of philosophy an exhibitionistic, immodest subjectivity. I have the impression that the seductiveness of the later Heidegger for us, and also the attractiveness of neo-Hegelianism and Marxism, perhaps even of structuralism, comes—in part of course—from a reaction to that completely naked subjectivity that, in its desire to avoid losing itself in the universal, rejects all form.

The second point. It is Kierkegaard's violence that shocks me. The manner of the strong and the violent, who fear neither scandal nor destruction, has become, since Kierkegaard and before Nietzsche, a manner of philosophy. One philosophizes with a hammer. In that permanent scandal, in that opposition to everything, I perceive by anticipation the echoes of certain cases of verbal violence that claimed to be schools of thought, and pure ones at that. I am thinking not only of National Socialism, but of all the sorts of thought it exalted. That harshness of Kierkegaard emerges at the exact moment when he "transcends ethics." Kierkegaard's entire polemics against speculative philosophy supposes subjectivity tensed on itself, existence as the care that a being takes for its own existence, and a kind of torment over oneself. The ethical means the general, for Kierkegaard. The singularity of the *I* would be lost, in his view, under a rule valid for all. Generality can neither contain nor express the *I*'s secret. Now, it is not at all certain that ethics is where he sees it. Ethics as consciousness of a responsibility toward others (Mlle Hersch[3] spoke well, just a short while ago, of the infinite requirement that calls you to responsibility without your being able to have yourself replaced), far from losing you in generality, singularizes you, poses you as a unique individual, as *I*.

Kierkegaard seems not to have experienced that, since he wants to transcend the ethical stage, which to him is the stage of generality. In his evocation of Abraham,[4] he describes the encounter with God at the point where subjectivity rises to the level of the religious, that is to say, above ethics. But one could think the opposite: Abraham's attentiveness to the voice that led him back to the ethical order, in forbidding him to perform a human sacrifice, is the highest point in the drama. That he obeyed the first voice is astonishing: that he had sufficient distance with respect to that obedience to hear the second voice—that is the essential. Moreover, why does Kierkegaard never speak of the dialogue in which Abraham intercedes for Sodom and Gomorrah on behalf of the just who may be present there?[5] Here, in Abraham, the precondition of any possible triumph of life over death is formulated. Death is powerless over the finite life that receives a meaning from an infinite responsibility for the other, from a diacony constituting the subjectivity of the subject, which is totally a tension toward the other. It is here, in ethics, that there is an appeal to the uniqueness of the subject, and a bestowal of meaning to life, despite death.

II

Thus Kierkegaard brings something absolutely new to European philosophy: the possibility of attaining truth through the ever-recurrent inner rending of doubt, which is not only an invitation to verify evidence, but part of evidence itself. I think that Kierkegaard's philosophical novelty is in his idea of belief. Belief is not, for him, an imperfect knowledge of a truth that would be perfect and triumphant in itself. In his view, belief is not a small truth, a truth without certainty, a degradation of knowledge. There is, in Kierkegaard, an opposition not between faith and knowledge, in which the uncertain would be set in opposition to the certain, but between truth triumphant and truth persecuted. Persecuted truth is not simply a truth wrongly approached. Persecution and, by the same token, humility are modalities of the true. This is something completely new. The grandeur of transcendent truth—its very transcendence—is linked to its humility. Transcendent truth manifests itself as if it did not dare to say its name, and thus as always about to leave. Thus it does not come to take its place among the phenomena with which it would be confused, as if it did not come from elsewhere. One may even wonder whether the Revelation, which expresses the origin of transcendental truth, is not contrary to its essence, given that transcendental truth can manifest itself authentically only as persecuted; one may wonder whether the *incognito* should not be the very mode of revelation—and whether the truth that has been said should not also appear as something about which nothing has been said.

The idea that the transcendence of the transcendent resides in its extreme humility allows us to glimpse a truth that is not a disclosure. The humility of persecuted truth is so great that it does not dare show itself "in the clearing" of which Heidegger has spoken. Or, if you like, its presentation is equivocal: it is there as if it were not there. Such is, in my view, the new philosophical idea contributed by Kierkegaard. The idea of persecuted truth allows us, perhaps, to put an end to the game of disclosure, in which immanence always wins out over transcendence; for, once being has been disclosed, even partially, even in Mystery, it becomes immanent. There is no true exteriority in this disclosure. Now, here with Kierkegaard something is manifested, yet one may wonder whether there was any manifestation. Someone began to say something—but no! He said nothing. Truth is played out on a double register: at the same time the essential has been said, and, if you like, nothing has been said. This is the new situation—a permanent rending, an ending that is no ending. Revelation—then looking back on it, nothing. This new modality of truth brought to us by Kierkegaard is not merely a philosopher's invention. It is truly the translation of an age (and what Beaufret[6] said yesterday about Kierkegaard's being the thinker of our time is absolutely true, but perhaps not solely for Heideggerian reasons) that has lost confidence in the historical authenticity of the Scriptures without having lost the possibility of hearing, through them, a voice from afar. The Scriptures—perhaps there is nothing to them. Since the historical criticism of the Bible, they can be explained by a great many contingencies. Yet there was a message. It is in this sense that there is, in the Kierkegaardian manner of truth, a new modality of the True.

10 Jean Lacroix: Philosophy and Religion

I

The gods, dwelling upon the world's heights, find their place in philosophical discourse. They retain it after their retreat into the mythical cities, as philosophical discourse invests the myths or takes refuge in them. The God of the Bible, whose ways are unknown, whose presence may be but absence and whose absence may impose itself as presence, to whom the faithful is both faithful and unfaithful, reveals himself in the interruption of coherent speech. And yet the Westerner, irreversibly a philosopher, does not consent to that separation between faith (or what is left of it) and philosophy. He desires a discourse capable of incorporating that interruption itself.

The discourse sought after is recognized as being rational only if the Greeks have fixed its vocabulary and syntax; so that no new notion accedes to philosophical dignity and is accredited unless it is defined in terms of that originary vocabulary and formed according to that syntax or logic. Doubtless the power of that language resides in its refusal of all *extrinsicality*, that is, in its virtue of extreme consciousness. Extreme consciousness, or consciousness more conscious than consciousness, which, despite the absolute vigilance in which it maintains itself, still obscures, with its thickness of individuality, the pure transparency of that shadowless noon, interiority. An extreme consciousness, i.e. a consciousness that is no longer subjectivity (that never was subjectivity): *logos*. Nothing stated by this *logos* can have crept in by stealth. Nothing gets in by having broken the chain of *logos*. For any new thing there must be a recollection. The *said* of this *saying* is a theme, in which whatever is posed becomes by the very fact exposed and proposed—appears, is present, *is*. It is a language attached to the phenomenon—to what shows itself, to something the very appearance of which is an evincing: being. It illuminates, with a pure white light, a space without hiding-places or corners, without clandestinity, without mystery; it draws into *one sole* totality, i.e. without transcendence. Phenomenality is the fact that *the thought that reaches being is the exact equivalent of the being open to thought.* An extreme or Western thought is an attention to facts—events and movements of the world—pushed to the point of perceiving itself as the pure intelligibility of these facts. It is only at this price that it is permissible to say that modern humanity is the power of "not accepting anything as being true" that one does not know "self-evidently to be so."[1]

Philosophical discourse, including that of Plato—whether deducible *a priori* from primary self-evidence, or in conformity with the categories that set its conditions, or based on the experience of a Nature that is one, ready to reveal itself, not rent by any miracle—already implies, by the form of its saying, the exclusion of worlds-behind-the-world.[2] In the Western tradition all philosophy, even a philosophy of transcendence, is reduced, as philosophical *logos*, to immanence. Beyond that formal immanentism, the end of metaphysics, which is on everyone's lips these days (though there is no agreement on the precise meaning of that end, nor on that of the word metaphysics), consists in keeping careful watch over what might be called the crypto-extrinsic within the *content* of notions into which clandestine elements may have infiltrated. They may have slipped in, as within a Trojan horse, shrouded beneath the impenetrable secrecy of some personal inner world, or the hermeneutics (however rational) of a myth.

The Nietzschean formula "God is dead" was not called to such great notoriety for having sanctioned or preached the disappearance of faith from among the important psychological factors in life. The scientific certainties that have replaced that faith are certainly not based, for most people, on the rational universality from which they proceed. Those beliefs are based on yet another form of faith: faith in the University, which (despite the protests) confers the right to speak, and in technology, which triumphs over matter with matter. But "God is dead" is the death, even at the University, of hermeneutics, the revelatory power of myth, fable, symbolic form; the death of letters sheltering the spirit, and of what one may call in a general, but also a very accurate way, the Holy Scriptures. By a strange privilege, some Olympian myths have resisted de-mythification, and, like the myth of Oedipus, preside over the process, suggesting new dimensions for reflection and providing "food for thought." But one no longer focuses on the exegesis of the Scriptures: one studies their genesis.[3]

Their cause, their formula, or their structure: these are studied, as if they were a part of the proliferation of ethnological facts. Ethnology is no longer one discipline among others. As a philosophy refusing all surprise (requiring that all facts be noted and incorporated), it begins in a universal exoticism which also envelops the civilization to which the investigator belongs—the civilization that provided the very means of assessment he or she employs at the frontiers of consciousness. Myths, henceforth, contain neither truth nor falsehood. They are social or psychic products, instruments of defense, dreams of resentment or satisfaction, images devoid of gnoseological value. One must not interpret them, but must explain them or take them as symptoms—never as symbols. Beware of the illusions that they can cause if their purely phantasmatic existence is taken for the meaning of the true.

Marx, Nietzsche and Freud are the masters of that philosophy that Ricoeur called the philosophy of suspicion, and in which Jean Lacroix has perceived the current religious challenge (if not crisis)—above and beyond all the errors fallen into by religious institutions, doctrines, methods and commitments, in an effort to become part of the established order. As a keen listener to all the nuanced expression of contemporary philosophical thought, Jean Lacroix certainly does not forget, in his observations, the social, economic and political conditions offered (or denied) to the religious consciousness of our time. But his main concern is with the philosophical sources of that crisis, as determined by, or reflected in, the teaching of a few prestigious masters of letters or the human sciences of today—the four, or five, or six great ones.

II

Does not the modern religious "consciousness," with its extreme sensitivity to the difference between apologetic discourse and discourse at the level of universality (though, paradoxically, that universality does not achieve a consensus approaching forecasts or tabulated results), abolish itself as consciousness? And do the quotation marks, which in modern writing too conveniently take the place of so many absent or impossible words, suffice to suggest the psyche for which *religious* should serve as adjective?

It is doubtless in order to try to resolve the crisis by aggravating it that we are invited, if not to return to Spinoza, at least to turn to him; to question Spinoza, who, in the context of today's French anti-humanism, as in that of Brunschvicg's[4] humanist idealism of the recent past, expresses philosophy's truth. This fascination is shared by Jean Lacroix with a great many of his contemporaries who are not interested in religion. Kant discovered the *transcendental appearance*, and indeed taught us to investigate the birth of a notion before adhering to its intentionality; he nonetheless caught sight, in the illusions of the transcendental dialectic, of the first glimmer of the practical *truths*. Hegel, for whom philosophy is the truth of Christianity, thereby fails to free himself from exegesis. Husserl's phenomenology is incapable of de-mythologizing the mind, for it enters into all intentions—possibly even those of madness. It is in

Spinoza that images—associated with knowledge of the first kind—receive from the second and third kind only an explanation, not a deepening.[5] Spinoza is the first messenger of the death of a God bearing the well-known resemblance to man spoken of in Genesis. The understanding of Scripture through Scripture, which is propounded in the *Theologico-Political Treatise*, means that it is forbidden to seek philosophical concepts in Scripture.[6] Scripture may be salutary, like truth—but it is not the latter's implicit prefiguration. It is not an infused wisdom, an interiority or a reason that is unaware of itself.

To seek in Spinoza a philosophy giving satisfaction to a soul that takes Scripture as its authority constitutes a daring project, despite the presence of God in the theorems of the *Ethics*, and Novalis's comment about Spinoza's being drunk with God. Jean Lacroix insists on the *in-humanist* discourse of Spinoza, as a philosopher of being, of being explaining itself by its unfolding. All anthropomorphism is excluded, all transference (even transposed to a superlative degree) of human powers or ends to God. The divinity of being or nature consists in the pure positivity of *esse*, in the very strength of its being, which expresses itself in the deductive engendering of *natura naturata*. This is an unsurpassable force or rationality, for there is nothing beyond that positivity and that *conatus*, no value in the sense of a surpassing of being by the good; it is a totality without *beyond*, affirmed perhaps more deeply than in Nietzsche himself—a totality that is but another name for the non-clandestineness of being, or for its intelligibility, in which inner and outer coincide. Within the rigor of this order—necessary without heteronomy—there is a place for man, who is the mode of an attribute (and not the cherished son of the father), and who, engulfed but not absorbed, is at a distance from this God according to a transcendence that knowledge of the third kind (understanding his place as mode in the substance) allows to be internalized. The spirit of this interiority would not stifle the respiration of the Christian soul, unencumbered by all the extrinsicality in which the political reaction enclosed the doctrine of the Gospels. A philosophy without axiology in which all the threatened values reappear, derived from Being: liberation from enslavement to the passions, the re-education of desire, disalienation, love of one's neighbor. A liberal state. The intellectual love of God and the eternity He opens to the philosopher, who receives from God the very love he bears Him—these are not a dissolution into anonymity, and would not be unworthy of the salvation promised to the elect. Let us note, on the subject of this interpretation of Spinozism, to what a great degree the religious tradition of the West has maintained an equivalence or at least an indisputable kinship between spirituality and knowledge.

But the very rationality of the Spinozan order requires that the path to salvation be open to all men, even if they are unable to rise to a knowledge of the third kind. Beginning with representations of an order inferior to the True, they can be prompted to the love of God and of their neighbor, and to virtue, and thus be saved according to the statutory religion of the Old and New Testaments. This would assume the purely spiritual event of the conferment—upon a man worthy of the adjective divine, and one who is "more than a philosopher"—of a perfect knowledge of God, of a wisdom higher than wisdom and from which the biblical and, more especially, the Christian message would emanate.

III

Philosophy brought into harmony with faith, in what is essential in the latter according to the interiority of Reason and thus in a manner more convincing than any meditation on the religious experience—this is, it seems, the central nerve of Jean Lacroix's stern and fervent little volume. The two other publications, which appeared at the same time, anchor this project in the present.[7] But taken together they attest to a curious resurgence in religious modernism of a state of mind that we have perhaps not seen since Saint Thomas Aquinas.

The most lucid religious modernity continues to relate all *meaning* to the unity and totality of being. The religious significance of unenglobable transcendence surrounds itself with ontological guarantees. Faith runs no risks without reassuring itself; the existence of God is the first problem, without which the rest would be but rhetoric. Despite the phrase—also of Greek origin—about the Good beyond being,[8] it is *to be* that counts. The discourse, as confirmed by Hegel in its divine nature, that gathers into one universal theme and synchronizes in one historical vision the absolute diachrony of transcendence, remains master of all things. Philosophy drives out metaphysics.

But does there not exist for modern consciousness (without its having to accuse itself of anachronism) an alternative that does not come down to a choice between reason and an incommunicable meaning, between theology and mysticism? A God identical with absolute being, thus existing beyond all measure, filling in the shortcomings and breaks in man's relative being with His positivity of being, within the closed circuit of totality: such would be the first term of the alternative, in the background of which Spinozism may be discerned. And at this pole is to be placed (though it be only in anguish) the existentialist thought of the recent past, fearing, in the consciousness of its ontological failure, that the heavens may be empty, or that being may be finite.

But does not transcendence reawaken behind the walls that claim to protect it? The work of a Blanchot, for example, is the fact (and not merely testimony to the fact) that totalized totality does not absorb a scurrying about, or a dull, monotonous moan of silence that sets in. As if the totality would not settle down in order. A monotony that is not a *logos*: neither the anguish of the rational animality of the subject struggling within the confinement of his finitude, nor his astonished wonder at the extraordinary reign of order. Nothing short of a consciousness of the totality, to which that consciousness, moreover, already belongs; the *ennui* that becomes literature and continually works at self-delusion or at silencing that endless drone of silence, or that nothingness that "nothings"[9] instead of being still—as a good nothingness should do.

Transcendence, in contemporary poetry (but probably perennially), may disrupt and bewilder *apophansis*,[10] which is unable to embrace its *epos* in terms that, delayed in relation to their writing [*écriture*], do not rejoin their identity.

Or, beyond these events—too casually taxed with nihilism—transcendence may burst forth in the daring attempt to transform the world after having understood it, in response to the obsession exerted on the *order* by a humanity that is not yet "in order," or the order of which, ever in question, constantly weighs upon my responsibility as a hostage.

Or transcendence may be a proximity of the neighbor that can be reduced neither to truths nor to contiguity—beyond "gathering together." "I opened to my friend—he is lost—he has passed."[11]

Literature, writing [*écriture*], ataxia, audacity, proximity: these are not experiences of literature, disorder, or proximity. Experience would still be knowledge, still opening on being, already ontology, already philosophy, already totalization. Transcendence arises again, from behind every experience of transcendence, which tries to surround, circumscribe or circumvent, fasten or bind, transcendence. For this binding, the cord is not too short, or too frayed. But the concern here is with meanings that arouse totally different shivers[12] of the human.

From the depths of the muddy, miasmatic swamps, from among these diastases of identity, and from these desertions from Order (which are not merely disturbances of the established order), can the name of God resound? *Pure* transcendence cannot interrupt totalization *in any other way*. Placing another Being beyond the totalized totality, however high, would not prevent its immediate agglutination to the totality it transcends—despite the distance that the simple *unity of analogy* interposes. Such is the infrangible destiny of being: of *esse*, of *Sein*. But pure transcendence does not lead to the Singular Name in a manner any more arbitrary than the neuter notion of "necessary being," or of "substance that is in itself and is conceived through itself."[13] It is not necessary and it is not possible for this name to resound in being through demonstrations or actuality, nor for its "kingdom" to be manifestation and miracle. The youthfulness of its transcendent meaning does not signify in beliefs or hopes, but in the excessive expenditure of the human, in *the-one-for-the-other*, destroying the balance of accounts; in the "meaningfulness freely bestowed," without expectation of thanks, in the hyperbole exceeding long life and eternity. A project that moves not in the direction of being or non-being, but toward an excluded middle; even if language states it as *a being* or as *being*, in calling it God. Language, ambiguous *per se* (ancillary and indiscreet), that betrays the ineffable, but thus revealing it and offering it to the "reduction" of metaphysics.

This second term of the alternative, which consists in thinking a risky transcendence or in risking transcendence, is not a romantic eventuality. It is the moving force behind today's humanity. It is the other side of an anti-humanism that denies the *I* that takes its own security for an ontology. But the *I* is still itself and not an other—different from all the others and unique—inasmuch as, having set its sovereignty aside, it makes itself responsible for freedoms foreign to its own, as non-indifferent to others, and, precisely thus, as absolutely different. An existence relative indeed, of one-for-the-other, a substitution and signifyingness [*significance*] of the sign. An excessive expenditure if there ever was one, in the responsibility of the *one* reduced to the condition—or incondition—of hostage to all the *others*.

These notions imply the heteronomy of an obligation going beyond commitments freely made. They shockingly impugn the sacrosanct idea of autonomy. But does not the spiritualization to which autonomy was a response open up, with the depths of interiority, the dimension of the "all is permitted," a dimension in which the twists and turns, prepared in advance in mental reservations, run on as far as the eye can see—and in which Difference is lost, to the point of indifference of one for another, to the point of "no more whining or weeping"—but in which the totalization of being finds its ultimate resources to work itself up to totalitarianism? It is the long-term consequence of a spiritualization as much to be feared as the repressive extrinsical-ism of a Bonald or a Joseph de Maistre.[14]

M. Jean Lacroix formerly contemplated a philosophy of insufficiency, or a necessary insufficiency of philosophy, which was to leave a place for faith. He now believes that position untenable, and that one must, in philosophy, go on to the end, to Spinozism, without despairing of hearing within it (be it only in the form of variations) the interiority and salvation that are the life of religion. His venture is bold, subtle and nuanced. One may choose to pursue it. An insufficiency in philosophy would be just one more woe for philosophy, which as we know has been condemned without appeal. But can sufficiency appease a modern mind? In any case, sufficiency and self-satisfaction—which are the very hallmark of the commentators or tutors of several absolute ways of thinking (right down to their facile, epigonic irony), claiming to enclose transcendence within immanence—cannot reduce all dissident meaning to absurdity. No one is questioning the soundness of the knots they tie. No one wants to take advantage of the imperfections of the systems in order to add, by way of supplement, a knowledge devoid of reason.

But the significance and indisputable obligations that can be called religious (even if this term remains intolerable to certain people because of the puerilities it evokes)—significance and obligations that give meaning to an entire group of human beings who are responsible for others—may not adhere to the revolving, englobing movement of Greek philosophy. And the end of that philosophy, the escape from that encirclement, is not the end of the meaningful that a non-disseminated language, not encrusting its meaning in its syntax, might be able to say.

11 Roger Laporte and the Still Small Voice

We are witness to a singular intrigue. According to Laporte, the event *par excellence* is the word—the coming of meaning to being; and writing, a mode of meditation, allows the *event* to take place. But that meditation means the expulsion of the *I* outside its vessel or its skin, and, thus, transparency or pure receptivity. And that event, fleeting and uncertain, attests to the absolute exoticism of its presence by its way of being always about to leave, so that the good fortune of the visitation would be inseparable from the misfortune of imminent separation. The coming of a word that says nothing other than its coming, in a toneless voice. But to "write precisely" ["*écrire juste*"] it is necessary to have heard that word, whilst in order to hear it one must already "write precisely." A circle without exit or entrance. We do not know whether the word is a call or an answer. The distinctions and distances between subject and object are abolished. Writing, neither silence nor saying, but vigilance and waiting, is endowed with an inverted intentionality: it is a waiting for the unexpected and a desire the desirable does not fulfill but deepens.

What is related to us here is neither philosophy nor psychology nor a document. Rather unreflectively, a word on the book's cover classifies Roger Laporte's *Une voix de fin silence*[1] as a story. In it, all the above-mentioned contradictions follow upon one

i.e. exposure

in other words, Saying

note L's use of Blanchot's concepts

another, without being pacified in the form of a dialectic. But
this book, which perhaps would like to be no more than "precise
writing" in search of the event, belongs unquestionably by its
beauty to belles-lettres.

Maurice Blanchot opened literature to that new dimension, in
which real characters consume themselves in a zone of high
tension that is neither objective reality nor the field of consciousness. Perhaps for Blanchot himself it represents the after-death
or the impossible death. The common clock on which the
survivors read the hour of death of the others is, perhaps, the
greatest malice of the Great Watchmaker. In their own time, the
dying will never cease dying. Their time no longer flows into
common time. Their endless agony is that incessant rolling of
the sea of being that rises like nausea to the living or revives
language, incapable of stopping: literature of course, but sometimes poetry, when a way out appears, even if that emergency
exit is a false door or false window. But it is as if exteriority and
interiority were the locus of a more original or ultimate event
which, precisely thus, in the literal sense of that banal locution,
takes place. What event? And why should it have a right to be a
part of literature? And why is it called word [*parole*] and even
writing [*écriture*]?

Sometimes the event resembles that of being, or, giving the
word *being* [*essence*] the value of an abstract noun designating an
action, the event resembles the *being* of being [*l'essence* de l'être],
the famous Heideggerian *being of a being* [*être de l'étant*]. In
Blanchot, there occurs a kind of impersonal, neuter sifting of the
same things again and again, an incessant sound of coming and
going, an endless rocking, like a fundamental opacity that cannot even properly be called fundamental, since it founds nothing: chaos, biblical "unformed and void." Roger Laporte seems,
on this point, closer to Heidegger and Beaufret.[2] He speaks of
advent, of summit, while taking pains to separate these notions
from the noisy triumphs of the conquerors. This voice that
approaches in becoming more distant, like an echo or a rhyme,
hovers at the edge of silence and forgetfulness.

poetry in advance of theology

92

At other times the event is like a leaving of self, like the passage from the Same to the absolutely Other (which is no less thought-provoking than the being of beings!) of which Kierkegaard speaks so insistently, and Jankélévitch without touching it. The absolute Other is the discovery no sooner discovered than put in question—truth persecuted. A rebirth of uncertainty: this is the very mode according to which the Other can pass among us without becoming an old acquaintance of this world. In Jankélévitch, a glimpse of the absolutely other attenuates the quiddity of what it surprises to the point of reducing it to the bare fact of fulguration, the flash of the glimpse itself.

How does all this concern letters? What is literature, if not this disproportion between writing and the work, if not this "meaning-bearing language" that comes to be superimposed upon the meaning that the author "thought he was putting into the words?" Is it not to those words that those who claim to be their lovers, the philologists and historians of letters, want to get back, as if to drive out the event? As if their main concern were to show nothing ever happened in writing outside the thoughts and emotions of the authors! In that obstinacy of modern literature, set on relating its own adventure, it would be easy to see a search for compensation for the frustrations of a lost faith. In reality what is at issue is the need for the absolute (could one desire less?) which traditional theology, with its mighty and (to Simone Weil's[3] great outrage) magical supernatural, with its beyond as simply presented as a landscape through the window, with its transcendence that can be stepped over like a fence, has too long failed to recognize. And to bring about the recovery of a worn-out theology, it does not suffice to proclaim that transcendence belongs *essentially* to subjectivity. The abusive use of this adverb defines, perhaps, the pseudo-thought of our time. Like the lead with which certain dolls were weighted in our childhood so they would imperturbably right themselves, the *I's self* [*le soi-même du Moi*] always sets it back on the same ground, in the same position, after all its metamorphoses. In our travels we

Literature as a desire for transcendence which theology merely packages)

take ourselves along. Now, through the literature of literature, with all "that business about language" all our childish mysteries and our fears are called into play again, and also the *I* is turned upside down.

Is language a listening that perceives or a contact that brings close? Manifestation and disclosure, or communication and proximity of the neighbor and ethical event irreducible to disclosure? These questions cannot be avoided. But it is around language, which in precise writing makes no noise and is no longer servile, that an important issue is being decided. One might question this privilege of writing, on which Roger Laporte writes subtle pages. But what does it matter? Reduced to its essence, language is perhaps the fact that one sole word is always proffered, which does not designate a being that is thought, but accomplishes a movement beyond being, and beyond the thought in which being looks at and reflects itself. More precisely, the proffering itself moves beyond thought. Saying [*Le dire*] is delirium [*est délire*]. Thought straightaway denounces that extravagance or verbalism, and, opposing words with the stones it wrests from their foundations, imprisons them in the world they mean to go beyond. Thought forces them to speak coherently. But in so doing once again the beyond, listened to by the daring of those poetic words, is told—and that communication "felt as the thing communicated itself," that "pure confiding." The transcendent cannot-*qua* transcendent—have come unless its coming is contested. Its epiphany is ambiguity or enigma, and may be just a word.

Language is the fact that always one sole word is proffered: God.

12 Max Picard and the Face

I

I corresponded with Max Picard for a few years, and I have read his works. I never met him, but have the impression of having seen his face. To me, to speak of Max Picard is almost like evoking an *apparition*, but one that is *strangely real.* That is perhaps the very definition of a poetic experience.

I have reread his letters—those postcards on which he wrote a few sentences in French and went on in German; often breaking off the French in mid-sentence to complete it in his native tongue. There is nothing in our exchanges that resembles a correspondence written with the intent of future publication. And our relationship was neither old enough nor deep enough to justify long intellectual confidences. But with Max Picard *one had the impression that the contact he kept up with you was even more important than the content it communicated,* that the voice was as important as the message. His whole self was there in person, facing yours. Not that relationships based on the participation of persons in a universal order are not generally at least as authentic as the attention they may direct toward one another. *But in exceptional people that attention is incomparably acute.* It bears no likeness to an outburst of emotion. It has the purity of a concept and the chastity of a motion of the mind.

II

Perhaps that is what it is that Picard's works impart. An interest in man, assuredly. But who would feel free, these days (despite the "crisis of humanism"), to say he was not interested in man? In Picard, *beyond an interest in man, there is an interest in each human face.* A philosophy of the face—that is the essential of Max Picard's thought. *The face is not just another name for the personality.* The face is the personality—but in its manifestation, its externalization and reception; in its original frankness. The face is of itself, and, if I may express it so, the mystery of all clarity, the secret of all openness.

That is why Picard uses the biblical expression according to which man is created in the image of God. And according to one of Max Picard's expressions, told to me by his son Michael, *the face of man is the proof of the existence of God.* Clearly the concern here is not with deductive proof, but with the very dimension of the divine (the monotheistic divine) disclosing itself in that *odd configuration of lines that make up the human face.* It is in the human face that—beyond the expression of human singularity and perhaps because of that ultimate singularity—*the trace of God is manifested, and the light of revelation inundates the universe.*

The personality in the *face* is at once the most irreplaceable, the most unique, and that which constitutes intelligibility itself. Through the human face conceived in the image of God, the universe becomes a plastic form; the teeming particles *take on* a meaning, crystallizing into an image, *into initial metaphors at the level of bare sensibility,* an original language, a primordial poem. Hence throughout Picard's work there are essays on physiognomy that consist not in seeking traits of psychological characteristics based on the lines of the human face, but in *deciphering the universe from these fundamental images or metaphors,* human faces: those we encounter in everyday life; those which, in their contact with eternity, we improperly call death masks; those which, having becoming portraits, observe us from the walls of museums.

III

How is this language to be deciphered? Only poetry can correspond to poetry. Picard's philosophical analysis is a poetic analysis. His reading of faces and the world is not always conceptually justifiable, nor phenomenologically convincing. It is poetically certain. In reading it one often thinks of the Bachelard[1] of the elements—Water, Air, Earth and Fire. One thinks of Bachelard who was his friend.

But one is especially justified in wondering whether the reading of first meanings can be other than poetic. Are we not dealing here with interpretations in which the first vocables and the first metaphors are constituted on the hither side of the coherent discourse of philosophers—vocables and metaphors without which such discourse would not even be possible? Does not language begin in that preliminary region in which the correspondences Baudelaire speaks of echo back and forth?[2] Do not the first words have their latent birth in the bringing of things closer to one another, which only then creates resemblances? Are not the fundamental theses on which systems will later rest first imperiously woven like poems, though their unjustifiable poetry be forgotten in the schools?

Picard describes for us, for example, in one of the admirable texts in his little book entitled *Monde du silence* [World of Silence], the time that flows by silently, the silently revolving rhythm of the seasons, as things and beings, leaves, flowers, fruits, colors, even noises, silently come out from the fissures of a silent flow, and suddenly are there. (This is no slow and heavy maturation, but a creative upsurge.) There, snow (and we must think of Swiss landscapes) is visible silence, bordered by the earth and sky. The silence of time? Time, in its noiseless flow, would be the native place of silence. But, one may say, what a plethora of metaphors! How arbitrary! The snow, a visible silence or the silence of time's flow? But who was the first person to say that time flows? And who first named time itself? In whose language could invisible time have become a substantive?

[margin handwritten note: poetry as language on the hither side of, philosophic Discourse]

IV

Max Picard's attitude toward the modern world—a world of noise; a world of beings and things that, in his view, have lost their faces, and one which modern art expresses (this broken world of which Gabriel Marcel has so admirably spoken)—Picard's attitude toward that world is one of rejection. This can be no surprise to us. But Max Picard's rejection of the modern world takes a form that contrasts sharply with the fad of the times, the "say no to technology" and to technocracy—which is communicated, as if by chance, through the press and radio, media through which this *no* participates in the modern world, from which it claims to separate itself.

Picard thinks nature, prior to any human intervention, bears more human meaning than the order which has come from human activity, worry and turmoil; he thinks that that meaning (or that silence) is necessary to man. That meaning is silence and not verb may be one of Picard's fundamental insights. The sublimity of Swiss landscapes removes from this anti-modernism any aftertaste of provincialism, conservatism and reactionary spirit. But above all, the order of nature is singularly close, in his view, to that of the face, of the word of God, which silently reverberates, so to speak, on these heights, on these forests, snows and lakes. Between the exile of the city dweller and the enrootedness of pagans drunk with the soil and the blood, there is a place (but absolutely non-Heideggerian) that comes from the word of the creator in Genesis. But Picard also thinks—and in this I scarcely dare to follow him—but then why do I keep the name God in my vocabulary?—Max Picard thinks man can dissociate himself from the evil that threatens his silence and his world with violence. A few months before his death, I received a little story of about twenty lines that doubtless relates the manner in which Picard passed among us.[3]

Someone is walking along beside a wood. There is a murderer in it. The passerby pays no attention to him, for he is telling himself his own story. The murderer can do nothing. It is as if his victim's inattention separated him from the world of crime, and did not leave to the homicidal gesture the moment necessary for the act of murder—the instant that murderer and victim have in common.

As if the throbbing in the killer's and the victim's temples might never be in phase. On his way back, the passerby sees the murderer again, still at the edge of the wood, and still incapable of killing. As if in his personal story—on condition that he leave no moment empty—the man found refuge from contemporaneity itself.

As if in his inner peace—on condition that it have meaning—he could paralyze the arm of the violent, and cause weapons to fall from their hands.

13 The Other in Proust

The eternity of the masterpieces does not wrest them free from time.

The present—unaware, capricious—seeks justification and foundation in the works of the past, which, though completed, thus take on new meaning, are revitalized and live. Proust, who no longer belongs to the present, since he can already guide it, enjoys the fabulous fate of countless afterlives.

What was he to the readers of the period between the two world wars, who, around 1933, tempted by an entire literature of heroism, action and rural nostalgia, were beginning to forget him? A master of the differential calculus of souls, a psychologist of the infinitesimal. A magician of inexpressible rhythms. One who, by a linguistic miracle, rediscovered and re-created a world and a time that had been lost in the scattering of instants. An emulator of Freud and Bergson, he posed futile problems of influences (the equivalent of canonization itself) for the critics. The aroma of the madeleine dipped in camomile tea was already pervading dusty textbooks, and served as a viaticum for students setting out for the unknown land of baccalaureate exams.

There was also Proust the sociologist. The new Saint-Simon of a nobility *sans* Versailles, the analyst of a world of preciosity and artificiality, a world frozen in history, caught up in conventions more concrete than reality itself; a world that (remarkably) offers its inhabitants, by its very abstractions, those dramatic and profound situations that, in a Shakespeare or a Dostoevsky, probed the humanity of man.

We have not changed all that. But the meticulousness of the analysis that once filled us with awe now no longer seems to us valid in itself; and the "explanations" that often in Proust's work are added to the analysis do not always convince us. It is doubtless to these "theories," these reasonings on the mechanism of the soul, so abundant in *Remembrance of Things Past*, that Sartre's remark of 1938 applies: "Proust's psychology? It is not even Bergson's: it's Ribot's."[1] That judgment, though harsh, reflects in any case the disrepute into which a whole aspect of Proust's work fell in the eyes of a generation that had been brought up on it.

But a disrepute that takes us to the essential. The theory of the scientist or philosopher is unequivocally related to the object that is its theme. The poet's theory (and everything he or she says) contains a hidden ambiguity, for it is a question not of expressing but of creating the object. Reasoning, like images or symbols, is meant to produce a certain rhythm in which the reality sought after will magically appear. The truths or errors stated do not count independently. They are spells and incantations. To discern within Proust's psychology the forces of empirical psychology is not to break, but to succumb to, the spell of Proust's work, in which theory is but a means.

It is obvious that this ambiguity is the very light that bathes Proust's poetry. The contours of the events, persons and things, despite the accuracy of delineation, the sculpting of personality traits and characters, remain in total indeterminacy. To the very end we will not know, in this world that is nonetheless our own, historically and geographically determined, exactly what took place. A world that is never definitive—a world in which realization does not sacrifice virtuality. The latter presses at the gates of being, and, like Banquo's ghost, sits down in the king's place. Like thoughts that carry with them a dimension of "second thoughts," actions also have their "second actions," with unforeseeable intentions, and things their "second things," in unsuspected perspectives and dimensions. This is the true interiorization of the Proustian world. It is not the result of a subjective vision of reality, nor even of the inner coordinates to which events, disdaining all objective points of reference and seeming to spring out of nowhere, correspond. Nor is it due to any metaphysical basis that might be sensed behind the allegorical, symbolic, or enigmatic appearances. It arises, rather, from the very structure of the appearances, which are at once what they are and the infinity of what they exclude. This is the case of the soul itself, which, within the universe of formulable legalities and choices made for eternity, reverses itself to become an "outlaw," in a compossibility of opposites, an annulment of all choices. It is curious to note to what point Proust's amoralism introduces the maddest freedom into his universe, and confers the sparkle of virtuality upon definite objects and beings, their potential undimmed by definition. It is as if moral rules banished enchantments from the world more harshly than did the laws of nature—as if magic, like the fabled witches' sabbath, began as soon as ethics eased. The most incredible metamorphoses and evolutions of the characters occur as being the most natural, in a world reverting to Sodom and Gomorrah. Relations between mutually exclusive terms set in. All is dizzyingly possible. It is this movement of defined reality slipping free of its definition that constitutes the very mystery penetrating Proustian reality. A mystery having nothing of the nocturnal: it does not extend the world into the invisible. The power of being to be incomparably more than it is does not derive from I know not what symbolic function it would take on, nor from a dynamism that would unfold it into a becoming, but from its infinite sparkle under the reflective gaze. Reality enjoys the benefit of infinite auto-referentiality: whence all the bite of its realness. Joy, suffering, emotion: in Proust they are never facts that count in themselves. The *I* is already separate from its state, in the very intimacy in which it normally stands with itself, like a stick immersed in water, breaking while remaining whole.

Spiritual effort acts at the level at which the *I* must take up what was apparently so naturally already its own. In Proust, the true emotion is always the emotion of the emotion. The former communicates to the latter all its warmth, and additionally all its anxiety. Despite Lachelier's principle, which distinguishes pain from reflection on pain, one being painful and the other only true or false, Proustian reflection, dominated by a separation between the *I* and its state, imparts its own accent to the inner life by a kind of refraction. It is as if I were constantly accompanied by another self, in unparalleled friendship, but also in a cold strangeness that life attempts to overcome. The mystery in Proust is the mystery of the other.

[handwritten margin note: as also in many of Blanchot's récits]

The result is something unique in Proust, something unprecedented in literature. His analyses, even when reminiscent of Ribot (which is rare, Sartre notwithstanding), merely translate that strangeness between self and self which is the spur of the soul. The rarified atmosphere in which events take place gives an aristocratic air to even the most mundane matters, imparting to simple words, such as "I suffered" or "I took pleasure in," an immaterial resonance, marked with the nobility of a rare and precious social relationship. It is not the inner event that counts, but the way in which the *I* grasps it and is overcome by it, as if encountering it in someone else. It is this way of taking hold of the event that constitutes the event itself. Hence the life of the psyche takes on an inimitable vibrancy. Behind the moving forces of the soul, it is the quiver in which the *I* grasps itself, the dialogue with the other within the self, the soul of the soul.

In this sense, Proust is the poet of the social; but not at all as the depictor of mores. The emotion elicited by a reflection on an emotion is completely within that reflection. Places and things move him through other people—through his grandmother, through his past self. The knowledge of what Albertine is doing, what Albertine is seeing and who is seeing Albertine has no intrinsic interest as knowledge, but it is infinitely exciting because of its deep strangeness in Albertine—because of that strangeness that laughs in the face of knowledge.

The story of Albertine as prisoner and as having disappeared, into which the very voluminous work of Proust launches, and all that searching down the tangled pathways of "Lost Time," is the narrative of the inner life's sudden intensification brought about by an insatiable curiosity about the alterity of the other, at once empty and inexhaustible. The reality of Albertine is her evanescence in her very captivity—a reality made up of nothingness. She is a prisoner, though she has already disappeared, and she has disappeared though a prisoner—since despite the strictest surveillance she retains a dimension of secrecy. The objective facts Proust is able to gather about her after her death do not dispel the doubt that surrounded her when her lies disguised her fugues. When she is no longer there to defend her absence, when evidence abounds, leaving no room for doubt, the doubt remains intact. Albertine's nothingness uncovers her total alterity. Death is the death of other people, contrary to the tendency of contemporary philosophy, which is focussed on one's own solitary death. Only the former is central to the search for lost time.[2] But the daily death—and the death of every instant—of other persons, as they withdraw into themselves, does not plunge beings into an incommunicable solitude: that is precisely what nurtures love. That is Eros in all its ontological purity, which does not require participation in a third term (tastes, common interests, a connaturality of souls)—but direct relationship with what gives itself in withholding itself, with the other *qua* other, with mystery.

The theme of solitude, of the basic incommunicability of the person, appears in modern thought and literature as the fundamental obstacle to universal brotherhood. The pathos of socialism crumbles against the eternal Bastille in which each of us remains his or her own captive, and in which we find ourselves when the celebration is over, the torches gone out and the crowd drawn back. The despair of the impossible communication, which fills (for example) Estaunié's[3] "solitudes"—rather unjustly forgotten—marks the limit of all pity, all generosity, all love. In short, collectivism shares this same despair. It seeks a term outside persons, in which each person will participate independently in order to blend into a community—impossible one on one. An ideal, a collective representation, a common enemy: these will unite individuals who cannot touch one another, cannot suffer one another.

But if communication thus bears the sign of failure or inauthenticity, it is because it is sought as fusion. One sets out from the idea that duality should be transformed into unity—that the social relation should end in communion. This is the last vestige of a conception identifying being and knowing—that is, the event by which the multiplicity of the real ends up referring to one sole being, and by which, through the miracle of clarity, everything I encounter exists as having come out of myself. The last vestige of idealism. The failure of communication is the failure of knowledge. One does not see that the success of knowledge would in fact destroy the nearness, the proximity, of the other. A proximity that, far from meaning something less than identification, opens up the horizons of social existence, brings out all the surplus of our experience of friendship and love, and brings to the definitiveness of our identical existence all the virtuality of the non-definitive.

Marcel did not love Albertine, if love is a fusion with the other, the ecstasy of one being before the perfections of the other, or the peace of possession. Tomorrow he will break with the young woman, who bores him. He will take that trip he has been planning for a long time. The story of Marcel's love is laced with confessions apparently designed to put in question the very consistency of that love. But that non-love is in fact love; that struggle with the ungraspable, possession; that absence of Albertine, her presence.

Thus the theme of solitude in Proust takes on a new meaning. Its event is in its conversion into communication. Its despair is an inexhaustible source of hope. A paradoxical conception, in a civilization that, despite the progress made since the Eleatics, sees in unity the very apotheosis of being. But Proust's most profound teaching—if indeed poetry teaches—consists in situating the real in a relation with what for ever remains other—with the other as absence and mystery. It consists in rediscovering this relation also within the very intimacy of the *I* and in inaugurating a dialectic that breaks definitively with Parmenides.

14 Father Herman Leo Van Breda

In 1938, German National Socialism was in full swing. It had been "destined" (but who would believe it today, and who wants to remember it) to rule the world, ushering in a millennium of a new civilization that would quite simply cancel out (*vertilgen*, not merely *aufheben*) the civilization of the previous two millennia. That destiny and that announcement had been made credible to the masses and, of course, to the "intellectuals" by a successful politics conducted with neither resistance nor mistakes, beginning in 1933. The fact that then, in that year of 1938, a young Belgian Franciscan was able to believe in the importance of Reason, whose days apparently were being counted even as she herself counted her evidences, losing them and seeking them once again in the depths of the wardrobes in which Husserl's manuscripts lay (themselves threatened with destruction in the house of Edmund Husserl's widow—a house deserted, abandoned by colleagues and students of philosophy)— that fact gives us a way to measure the lucidity, courage, heart, philosophical spirit and rationalism of Father Herman Leo Van Breda. He died suddenly at the age of sixty-three in Louvain, on the third of last March [1973].

The story of how the Husserl manuscripts were saved is well known. Father Van Breda used to relate it readily, and without smugness—but always with that good-humored laugh that his friends know so well and can hear in the article in which he tells the story. They hear it in his other stories as well. His kindness and academic subtlety were always seasoned, in this laugh, with a sprig of peasant guile, happy to have put one over on the devil. Well known also is the way Father Van Breda built the Husserl Archives of Louvain, with those 40,000 pages of shorthand by the master of phenomenology: with his thought of every waking moment, seemingly effortless ability, the optimistic intelligence of an organizer, the very sure knowledge of a scholar who had mastered the mass of thoughts he then went on to organize, classify, sort, edit and make available to the public; and with the authority of a leader who (despite his friendship with them) ruled over the co-workers whom he found thanks to a remarkable flair, workers who have become or are becoming masters in their own right. That knowledge was demonstrated by Father Van Breda in his still unpublished thesis of 1941, on the "Transcendental Reduction in the Later Husserl (1920–1938)," and in studies and notes scattered in the journals, and in the lecture given in January of 1973 to the Société française de philosophie, published in the present Bulletin,[1] which was probably intended to preface a broader project. That authority and love of people made it possible for Father Van Breda to organize international meetings and congresses successfully, and so contribute to bringing about that intersubjective concordance of thoughts that constituted, in Husserl's eyes, truth's proper mode of being. He had this goal of mutual understanding in mind already at the First International Colloquium on Phenomenology held in Brussels in 1952. France, England, the Netherlands, Italy, Switzerland, the United States, and of course Belgium were represented. German phenomenologists whom the Father knew to be untainted by Hitlerism—Eugen Fink, Ludwig Landgrebe and Max Müller—entered into discussion with (to mention only those coming from France) Koyré, Merleau-Ponty, de Schloezer, Jacques Havet, Ricoeur, Jean Wahl and Eric Weil. A precocious reconciliation? These were people who had never been estranged. And they relied on Father Van

Breda. Just as in 1938 he kept his composure in the face of news of Hitler's victories, and just as from 1940 to 1944, during the occupation, he protected the persecuted, so he would keep a cool head and a keen phenomenological ear to the end: always on the lookout for anything suspect, capable of discerning the howling of wolves in the seduction of discourse. His choices were sound, his friends the friends of his friends. The hardship of illness and the periods of discouragement he had to get through during the last years of his life did not let misanthropy diminish his openness to others. His friends retain moving memories of the fact. But must we pursue the path of memoirs before a tomb so recently closed? May this reminder of his unfailing faithfulness to great, just causes and his objectively visible work suffice.

In that old town of Louvain where philosophers, deepening medieval thought, never intended to turn their backs on the contemporary world, Father Van Breda was able to open a window to what is most valid today—whether in the form of research or debate—in a world athirst for rigorous knowledge and justice. Husserl's phenomenology, as I have already had occasion to say, has brought to contemporary thought, and even to the disciplines (and indisciplines) suspicious of the "transcendental subject," a new attentiveness to things, without which the so enlightening formalisms would have foundered in tautology.

But Father Van Breda has, in a way, had a hand in that philosophy's very destiny, giving it a second life, very soon after the death of the philosopher himself, when the most outstanding works, upon the death of their creators, undergo that eclipse called purgatory. The Husserl Archives were conceived as a wellspring of life, a rallying-point for scholars (at Louvain, and other academic centers under the authority of Louvain)—a visiting scholars' residence, above any sectarianism; a program of work to be carried out, a center for the publication of critical editions of Husserl and phenomenological studies (*Husserliana* and *Phaenomenologica*, the admirable series by the Martinus Nijhoff publishing firm in The Hague).

But Father Van Breda has also brought to light the reluctant portion of Husserl's first life. The manuscripts found in the form of finished works, but which Husserl would not, due to some ultimate, impassible and mysterious scruple, allow himself to publish (*Ideen II* and *Ideen III*, in particular), suddenly came out, casting a new light upon, or finding new enigmas within, the previously published works. And then the founder/director of the Husserl Archives brought out of secrecy Husserl's thought at the research stage, by publishing, or making available in the form of typewritten transcripts, courses, or notes, a thinking that was still trying itself out on paper. These "rough draft thoughts" and held-back books—late births—surrounded the work that had been published during the philosopher's lifetime like a thick atmospheric layer or a giant halo. "The globe of the world seems to float in a subjective milieu," writes Husserl in *La Psychologie phénoménologique*.[2] The way philosophy has emerged from the unpublished manuscripts since Van Breda's work resembles the transcendental constitution (in a consciousness that left the world in 1938) of that transcendental philosophy itself. The decisive moment represented by phenomenology in Western thought is worthy, by its opening out upon the non-said, of the meaning it has disclosed to our modernity.

15 Jean Wahl and Feeling

Sensibility is enjoying greater esteem in contemporary thought. It no longer appears as a stammering thought, condemned to error and illusion, nor even as a mere spring board for rational knowledge. Under the influence of Bergson, but especially of phenomenology, sensibility is seen to possess its own specific depth and wisdom. All intellectual construction receives the style and the very dimensions of its architecture from sensible experience—which it claims to transcend. We must revisit this original experience, this "pre-predicative" infrastructure.

Certainly this is congenial to empiricism, but to a very new sort of empiricism. Sensibility does not simply register the facts; it sketches out something like the "vital statistics" and metaphysical destiny of the being experienced. The senses make sense. The loftiest works of the mind bear their indelible trace. One might also use the Kantian term, transcendental esthetics, as does Husserl. One might say that, for our contemporaries, the transcendental function of sensibility is to weave pure forms—other than those of space and time—from the tangled skein that is the very content of sensations. The way the forms of space and time mark the phenomenal object in Kantianism closely resembles the way a phenomenology of pre-predicative experience would render the scientific universe intelligible. The rehabilitation of sensibility I just mentioned goes back ultimately to Kant. Pure sensibility—that was his discovery. The importance thus granted to sensibility brings back and revives many memories. The anti-intellectualist themes appear to recur like the swing of a pendulum. Does Jean Wahl's treatise on metaphysics,[1] which touches on all the philosophical themes (often with the scrupulousness of a doxography) but gives to the faculty of feeling [*le sentir*] and to feelings [*le sentiment*] the last word, simply mark a phase that has already been lived through several times before? Does he not merely choose, subjectively, between the terms of one of those eternal alternatives before which the history of philosophy runs its wavering course? Is there a crisis of the intelligence? It is not more serious than the crisis of feelings. But Wahl, who has read all the books and everything valid (and sometimes even invalid) that has been said in philosophy, knows all this.

Does the rejection of systems, the recourse to intuitive enlightenment or to the density of feelings, mark the end of a century expiring at the age of fifty, opening onto a silence in which the ineffable mixes with the bad silence of stagnant waters? Is it the disarray of a social class? The end of a world? But this technique of seeking, behind discourse, the author's secret suffering and the social ills that, unbeknownst to him, are exerting their nefarious influence—this technique also leads to silence. It would reduce all words to symptoms, including the ones interpreting those symptoms. In reality, feelings, which recur in Wahl at the end of every chapter of his metaphysics, are presented as the source of a new spiritual life. It is not skepticism that these pages, howeve̤ well informed, convey. Beyond the didactic value of this metaphysical compendium, with an acuity rivaled only by the simplicity of the language used (consider, for example, the passages on the notion of existence in Kant), the work is important because of the problem it deals with. It does not affect us because it *prefers* one philosophical school to another; it responds to a torment to which history seems to lead: the alienation of man by that very universality that, since the dawn of our civilization, was supposed to ensure the humanity of man.

The European does not believe in the substance of man. A man who is poor, all by himself, with nothing outside himself, is a poor man. Unhappiness is a way for substance to be nothing. Man's supreme work—a broad, open, welcoming life—is accomplished in transcendence. Being is valued by him—more than for its immutable stability—for its exteriority. The sovereignty of the *I* is a dependency. The possession of self depends on a dominion over the elements, on property, recognition by others, friendships, services, consideration. Desire, which should have belied his mastery, exalts it. Exteriority not only supplies him with what he needs to appease his desire: he *wants* his desire, which opens up exteriority to him. Desire, the source of happiness, of existence above existence, is not a simple lack, a simple emptiness. The appetite for life increases and confirms man's existence. The "fruits of the earth"[2] can fulfill and uplift. European existence, in its forms most hostile to the world, has not desired to triumph over torturing, enslaving desire through poverty and self-deprivation. It has substituted true desire for false. As opposed to the reports of Asian wisdom that reached it, European existence overcame desire by satisfying it. Asceticism itself, which was at first a part of the training of athletes, is still practiced with an eye to some triumph and future glory. The contradictions and trials of a life of luxury are preferable, after all, to the degradation of poverty. The minimum of material goods called for by Aristotle for the happiness of the free man presupposes an identification between the free man and the satisfied man. Western moral thinking was materialist and realist long before Marx.

Actually it is not a question of materialism. European man seeks a basis in exteriority. In desire, he feeds on being, but, satisfied, is immediately cut off from it. He needs deeper foundations in being than the ephemeral satisfaction of desire—a relation with exteriority in which exteriority blends with his evanescent substance otherwise than as food. This relation with external being, in which the latter blends in with the subject's substance permanently, is possession. One must possess beyond what is held in the hand, beyond what one eats and uses every minute. A sort of astral body, made up of everything man owes, extends the biological body. The political animal! A society, a state and laws are needed, which would discern in this invisible body man's true surface. We must not, then, see property as insurance against the uncertainties of the future. There is, in the sort of property European man has always loved, an original tendency, differing from simple need. What is desired above all else is not the object owned, but the ownership of the object. That is why life does not just aspire to the securing of its needs. The goal of desire shifts, the ownership of the object is more important than its enjoyment, wealth is loved for its own sake, greed and miserliness are possible, and money loved. With money, my belonging to the world and the world's belonging to me merge. Money is property I can hold in my hands and hide; it is tied to my secret, it is my mystery, it mingles with my most intimate being. Plato's reduction of money to the love of pleasure in *The Republic* overlooks its metaphysical essence. In Europe, poverty and wealth are ultimately the measure of nothingness and being.

The mastery of self through the mastery of the universe is an integral part of European thought. It is through participation in ideas, which are *yonder*, that becoming can work toward a pale existence. From Plato to Hegel and even Heidegger, the thinker can only return to himself by completing a large circuit that takes him far from himself. He grasps himself in his objective concept, his act, his historical efficacy, his universal work. He *is* through the state. And all the rest is zoology. The *I* is determined at the heart of a totality, becomes itself in forgetting its uniqueness. The uniqueness of an individual, of a hunger, a need, a love—the child of indigence and abundance.

The critique of philosophical intellectualism enters into Jean Wahl's exposition wherever life turns into ideas that transcend it, shedding the keen immediacy and feeling of being. "We must

communicate substantially with what is substantial in things."[3]
"The substances that are the objects of thought can only be
relative."[4]

This conception of feeling concurs, on many essential points,
with Bergson's intuition. But our way of being Bergsonian
depends on the thinker whom we use as our Spencer. Clearly
Wahl's is Hegel. His presence, hostile or friendly, can be felt
throughout. "Philosophy, to me, is the quest for the immediate,"
Wahl says repeatedly. But for neither Bergson nor Wahl does the
immediate retain a formal meaning, as if a method directed
toward immediacy were to discover the fact of duration [*la
durée*]. To move to the immediate is already to become and to
last [*durer*]. Here the method is already the working of the being
it seeks. For Wahl, the movement going toward the immediate
does not stop at becoming. For him, the immediate becomes the
palpitation of a subjectivity and the descent into an absolute
interiority. Here is an example of that intimate itinerary.
"Quality seen in itself, or rather felt in itself, is interiority; from
outer interiority, which is that of color, for example, to inner
interiority, which is that of thought—or from that inner interiority to the still more intimate interiority which is its origin—we
continue to execute a movement of descent or perhaps of ascent
toward the ineffable."[5]

The aspect of feelings that Wahl is interested in is less their
affective warmth than a certain violence and intensity. Feeling is
something savage, dense, opaque, dark,[6] "blind, bare contact." It
is described as a jolt, a shiver, a spasm. As if the intensity of the
feeling constituted its content rather than its degree; as if the
essence of the feeling could be reduced to that tension, that contraction in which we could catch in the act the movement of
being toward its interiority, its descent into self.—A movement
radically opposed to transcendence: instead of losing or finding
itself in the universal, feeling, tensed on itself, affirms the inner
substance of man, or the personal structure of being. A philosophy of feeling opposed to Heidegger's. Feeling does not mark
our presence in the world, overcome by its own nothingness,

but marks the way in which we descend into, and concentrate ourselves on, ourselves.

Through this movement of contraction and interiorization, being is life. That which, being contradictory, bursts apart in language, is united in its tension in feeling: finite and infinite[7] and all the terms of the antimonies. United in feeling, these terms do not compromise feeling by their latent contradictions, but authenticate it by their tension. Wahl likes to quote Heraclitus, who compared life to an arched bow. Life cannot be transcended, but is turned "toward a future life on earth."[8] It cannot be grasped from outside, by means of ideas and works that would contain its true essence. By that release it would lose being. "It is still the body that triumphs over the body."[9] Sensible life (too lightly dismissed as "animal") is necessary in order for exteriority—concept, states and civilizations—to retain its living reality.

The intellectual act *par excellence*, realization, is release. "Distance from oneself in relation to oneself,"[10] consciousness is already a distantiation from the focal point of being and its burning, which it wants to recapture in its luminous but cold reflections. Does not the Platonic tendency "inherent in all intellectual philosophy" and "against which we must nevertheless struggle"[11] consist in positing the intelligible as an absolute, in placing in subordination to it the living intelligence that conceived it, and thus in seeking in the clarity of light the cause of the ardor of the flame?

This tension between opposites and not their reconciliation, a tension prior to becoming and to love, a tension at the heart of becoming and of love, this immediate consciousness of feeling— does it necessarily evoke the life of childhood, the lost paradise to which instinctive life clings? In Wahl's view, it is, in fact, adult, with all the maturity of our civilization. That contradiction of life contains echoes and premonitions of our distant odysseys, of our outer destinies. "There is, within us, this domain of feeling, through which we can grasp felt substances, and through which we can mingle with the universe."[12] But it is an affective expansion, that is, inseparable from our point of departure. "There are affective terms by means of which we can get back to primitive experience."

It is an experience that does not mean entering the cold world of eternal ideas or of impersonal history. The world rejoined is the lived world, which does not assume the part of the ultimate authority whose role it would be to justify man's existence. This is the meaning of the mysterious expression: to transcend transcendence toward immanence.

"Will the philosopher have the strength finally to transcend transcendence itself, and to fall valiantly into immanence, without letting the value of his effort toward transcendence be lost?" There we have an anti-intellectualism for the long-civilized—for those who have read Hegel. But at the end of the venture we will find "the point of departure, reappearing in its primitive form."[13] Feeling, once it has refused to embark on the ventures of the Idea, war and ownership, money and politics (the foundations of our being in Being, but also its alienation), will, through its dialectic of the "fragmentary," "singular pulsations" obeying a "logic of pure quality that would not enrich our view of the world," lead us toward a "bare, blind contact with the Other."[14] Bare, blind contact and a view that does not seek riches: this is a renewal of the theses of the Cynics.

In substituting feelings for the concept, Wahl opposes all traditional metaphysics from Plato to phenomenology, including Hegel and Marx. He is for the man disengaged from civilization and from the mediate. Heideggerian Being, like the Platonic idea, like the Hegelian concept, makes human being dependent on a transcendence, like the giant in the popular Russian fairy tale, whose heart beat from afar. Existing through civilization, the *I* becomes a concept. Cynicism refuses to think man in function of his work, the product of his hands, things, utensils. Man is not what he has made; he is distinct from the heritage he leaves behind, and in this sense is closer to nature than to the social. A kinship different from that of the great intellectual and economic traditions of our civilization. "The tradition of the *philosophia perennis* may have left some fundamental traits of human nature in the background, destroying to some degree the sense of our kinship with the universe, which has been better preserved in poetry,"[15] Jean Wahl writes at the beginning of his work. Diogenes[16] seeks man among the rubble of things. His lantern shines on the clutter of our closets, libraries, attics and museums.

To seek a homeland for oneself *outside*—in the realm of ideas and human works—all that is meaningful only in the final analysis as the life of feeling. "Ideas are valid only if they cease being ideas."[17] The validity of the dialectic is not in its synthesis, but in its affective essence, its drama: through all the mediations, immediate contact with the real is accomplished in the very contraction of feeling, "a bare, blind contact with the Other." Truth no longer consists in following our own shadow as it moves along the horizon of ideas, in identifying ourselves with our concepts or products, with the uniforms we wear, the objective role we play despite ourselves, with our social efficacy, our fortune, or our trade, with whatever we are for the psychoanalyst, the philologist, or posterity. To interpret truth as feeling is to relocate our being within ourselves, reconquering that heart that a supposedly immortal giant in Russian folklore had the privilege and the imprudence of keeping outside his body.

There is perhaps no greater contradiction in thought's returning with philosophy to the dark source of ideas in feeling than there is in following the movement of clear ideas into the sombre, apocalyptic perspectives in which modern science, the product of clear thinking, threatens humanity and its thinking with destruction. In opposition to the light of public life, in which the dreams and crises of the private man fade away like shadows— in opposition to history, in which the *I* is included only as a concept—it was only right that we should be reminded of the truth of the living man, the sensitive man, renewing cynicism's highest teachings. Man does not coincide with his works and

implements, nor with the heritage he has left. He does increas-
ingly resemble—by his works and implements—the impersonal
and coherent discourse that can be used in discussing him. But
he fits this discourse totally only in death.

16 Nameless

Since the end of the war, bloodshed has not ceased. Racism, imperialism and exploitation remain ruthless. Nations and individuals expose one another to hatred and contempt, fearing destitution and destruction.

But at least the victims know whither to lift their dying gaze. Their devastated areas belong to a world. Once again undisputed opinion, undisputable institutions and Justice exist. In discussion, in writing, in the schools, good has rejoined the Good of all latitudes, and evil has become the Evil of all time. Violence no longer dares speak its name. What was unique between 1940 and 1945 was the abandonment. One always dies alone, and everywhere the hapless know despair. And among the hapless and forlorn, the victims of injustice are everywhere and always the most hapless and forlorn. But who will say the loneliness of the victims who died in a world put in question by Hitler's triumphs, in which lies were not even necessary to Evil, certain of its excellence? Who will say the loneliness of those who thought themselves dying at the same time as Justice, at a time when judgments between good and evil found no criterion but in the hidden recesses of subjective conscience, no sign from without?

Interregnum or end of the Institutions, or as if being itself had been suspended. Nothing was official anymore. Nothing was objective. Not the least manifesto on the rights of Man. No "leftist intellectual protest"! Absence of any homeland, eviction from all French soil! Silence of every Church! Insecurity of all companionship. So these were "the straits" of the first chapter of Lamentations: "None to comfort her!", and the complaint of the Kippur ritual: "No high priest to offer sacrifices, nor any altar on which to place our holocausts!"

Over a quarter of a century ago, our lives were interrupted, and doubtless history itself. There was no longer any measure to contain monstrosities. When one has that tumor in the memory, twenty years can do nothing to change it. Soon death will no doubt cancel the unjustified privilege of having survived six million deaths. But if, during this stay of grace, life's occupations and diversions are filling life once more, if all the depreciated (or antediluvian) values are being restored, and all the words we thought belonged to dead languages are reappearing in newspapers and books, and many lost rights are again finding institutions and public force to protect them—nothing has been able to fill, or even cover over, the gaping pit. We still turn back to it from our daily occupations almost as frequently, and the vertigo that grips us at the edge is always the same.

Should we insist on bringing into this vertigo a portion of humanity whose memory is not sick from its own memories? And what of our children, who were born after the Liberation, and who already belong to that group? Will they be able to understand that feeling of chaos and emptiness?

Beyond the incommunicable emotion of that Passion in which all was consummated, what should or can one transmit in the form of a teaching twenty years later? Recall once more the difficult Jewish destiny and the stiffening of our necks? Exact a justice with neither passion nor statute of limitation, and be wary of a humanity whose progress is conditioned solely by its institutions and its techniques? No doubt. But we may, perhaps, draw from the experience of the concentration camps and from that Jewish clandestineness that has conferred ubiquity upon it, three truths that are transmissible and necessary to the new generation.

To live humanly, people need infinitely fewer things than they dispose of in the magnificent civilizations in which they live. That is the first truth. One can do without meals and rest, smiles, personal effects, decency and the right to turn the key to one's own room, pictures, friends, countrysides and sick leave, daily introspection and confession. We need neither empires nor purple, nor cathedrals, academies, amphitheaters, chariots, steeds: that was already our previous Jewish experience. The dropping away of all the forms between 1939 and 1945 reminded us, more than all the other symptoms, of the fragility of our assimilation. In that world at war, forgetful even of the laws of war, the relativity of all that seemed indispensable since we entered the city suddenly became apparent. We returned to the desert, a space without countryside, or to a space made to measure—like a tomb—to contain us; we returned to a space-receptacle. The ghetto is this, too, and not just separation away from the world.

But—the second truth (and it is also linked to a certainty and a hope of long ago): in crucial times, when the perishability of so many values is revealed, all human dignity consists in believing in their return. The highest duty, when "all is permitted," consists in feeling oneself responsible with regard to these values of peace. In not concluding, in a universe at war, that warlike virtues are the only sure ones; in not taking pleasure, during the tragic situation, in the virile virtues of death and desperate murder; in living dangerously only in order to remove dangers and to return to the shade of one's own vine and fig tree.

But—the third truth—we must henceforth, in the inevitable resumption of civilization and assimilation, teach the new generations the strength necessary to be strong in isolation, and all that a fragile consciousness is called upon to contain at such times. We must—reviving the memory of those who, non-Jews and Jews, without even knowing or seeing one another, found a way to behave amidst total chaos as if the world had not fallen apart—remembering the resistance of the maquis,[1] that is, precisely, a resistance having no other source but one's own certainty and inner self; we must, through such memories, open up a new access to Jewish texts and give new priority to the inner life. The *inner life*: one is almost ashamed to pronounce this pathetic expression in the face of so many realisms and objectivisms.

The Jewish Condition

When the temples are standing, the flags flying atop the palaces and the magistrates donning their sashes, the tempests raging in individual heads do not pose the threat of shipwreck. They are perhaps but the waves stirred by the winds of the world around well-anchored souls within their harbors. The true inner life is not a pious or revolutionary thought that comes to us in a stable world, but the obligation to lodge the whole of humankind in the shelter—exposed to all the winds—of conscience. And, truly, it is mad to seek out the tempest for its own sake, as if "in the tempest rest resided" (Lermontov). But the fact that settled, established humanity can at any moment be exposed to the dangerous situation of its morality residing entirely in its "heart of hearts," its dignity completely at the mercy of a subjective voice, no longer reflected or confirmed by any objective order—that is the risk upon which the honor of humankind depends. *But it may be this risk that is signified by the very fact that the Jewish condition is constituted within humanity.* Judaism is humanity on the brink of morality without institutions.

I do not mean that the Jewish condition is also an insurance against that risk. The Jews are a people like all other peoples; they, too, desire to know that the voice of their conscience is recorded in an imperishable civilization. They are an older, more skeptical people, more inquiring than the others, asking, before the others, whether that voice is not the echo of a historical order that transcends it. A people in love with happiness, like all peoples, and with the pleasures of life. But by a strange election, they are a people conditioned and situated among the nations in such a way (is this metaphysics or sociology?) that it is liable to find itself, overnight and without forewarning, in the wretchedness of its exile, its desert, ghetto or concentration camp—all the splendors of life swept away like tinsel, the Temple in flames, the prophets without vision, reduced to an inner morality that is belied by the universe. A people exposed, even in the most peaceful of times, to anti-Semitic remarks, because they are a people capable of discerning in such remarks a hiss beyond the range of common hearing. And already a chilling wind sweeps through the still decent or luxurious rooms, tearing down tapestries and pictures, putting out the lights, cracking the walls, reducing clothing to rags and bringing with it the screaming and howling of ruthless crowds. Anti-Semitic language unlike any other—is it an insult like other insults? An exterminating language, causing the Good, which glorified in Being, to return to unreality and crouch at the bottom of a subjectivity, chilled to the bone and trembling. A language that reveals to all Humanity, through the intermediary of a people chosen to hear it, a nihilistic devastation no other discourse could evoke. That election is indeed a hardship.

But that condition, in which human morality returns after so many centuries as to its womb, attests, with a very old testament, its origin on the hither side of civilizations. Civilizations made possible, called for, brought about, hailed and blessed by that morality—which can, however, for its part, only know and justify itself in the fragility of the conscience, in the "four cubits of the *Halakhah*," in that precarious, divine abode.

ON MAURICE BLANCHOT

1　The Poet's Vision　(1956)

1　Atheism and Inhumanism

Maurice Blanchot's reflection on art and literature has the highest ambitions. The interpretations of Hölderlin, Mallarmé, Rilke, Kafka and René Char he gives us in his most recent work[1] delve deeper than the most vigorous critique. The book is, in fact, situated beyond all critique and all exegesis.

And yet it does not tend toward philosophy. Not that its purport is inferior to such a thing—but Blanchot does not see, in philosophy, the ultimate possibility; nor, as a matter of fact, does he see in possibility itself—in the "I can"—the limit of the human. Everyone seems to think this century is the end of philosophy![2] This includes those who want to build a better world, to bring about change, and not just understand, as well as those who, at the other end of the spectrum, go back to the "truth of being" with Heidegger, to welcome its early morning rays, which will make the love of wisdom and its subdivision into disciplines pale in its light.[3] Contemporary thought holds the surprise for us of an atheism that is not humanist. The gods are dead or withdrawn from the world; concrete, even rational man does not contain the universe. In all those books that go beyond metaphysics we witness the exaltation of an obedience and a faithfulness that are not obedience or faithfulness *to* anyone. The absence of the gods translates into an indeterminate presence. A strange nothingness, that does not keep still but "nihilates;"[4] a silence gifted with speech, an essential speech, even. A faceless neuter, "*sans figure*,"[5] in Blanchard's phrase, even though a black light emanates from their [the absent gods'] anonymous, incessant movement. To the neo-Hegelian, as to Hegel, the human individual—the living subjectivity, conscious of itself in the immediate—cannot reflect the absolute. Historical reality is indeed reason, but a reason that does not shine forth at the very instant during which it subjugates wills and passions. It illuminates after the fact. Delayed self-evidence: that is perhaps the definition of the dialectic. The owl of Minerva does not spread its wings till dusk. In Heidegger, being, in the verbal sense he gives it, to distinguish it from beings (but everyone knows these distinctions in France), is the measure of all things, and of man. Man answers, or does not answer, its call. But a call that does not come from anyone. It comes from Being, which is not a being—from a phosphorescence of Nothingness, or, more precisely, from a luminosity in which the ebb and flow of Nothingness and Being continue on. Subjectivity's meaning does not come from itself, but from that phosphorescence, from the truth of being. As early as Aristotle, according to Heidegger, Western metaphysics had already forgotten that truth of being, forming "the image of the world" and progressing toward dominance through science. But all this—subject, forgetting of the truth of being, metaphysics, image of the world, science—is not the fault or caprice of man, but rather reflects the truth of being and its exigencies, even though man may be the very vocation of keeping watch over that truth; that is, vigilance and attention. History, while requiring man, is dependent on the fulgurations of being.

2 The Day and the Night

I have evoked the themes among which Blanchot's thinking moves. There is Hegel, who "does not speak lightly," announcing a reality regulated rationally by work and politics: behavior [*The Day*] Blanchot ranges under the categories of the Day. The Day is the World, Power and Action, and it embraces the whole range of the Human. Not including art, however, which accedes to a different space: Night. But above all there is Heidegger—the last Heidegger.

This may be said all the more freely, since Blanchot's first [*Blanchot as a late Heideggerian*] essays on the essence of art and literature, culminating in *L'Espace littéraire / The Space of Literature*, appeared at a time when the last Heidegger was totally unknown to the Heideggerians in France.[6] The affinity with the German philosopher can be felt in all kinds of ways; including Blanchot's choice of the texts of Rilke and Hölderlin to write on, and the (always masterful) way he employs analytic procedures that are characteristic of phenomenology (though perhaps these go back to Hegel) in which the irreducible physiognomy of notions reflects the originality of the itinerary leading to them. Beings and being are distinguished, and although Blanchot is pondering Mallarmé, who saw a mystery and a task to be completed in the little word "*c'est*" [it is], the accent with which the word *to be* is proffered is Heideggerian.

Blanchot situates the work of art, the poem, outside the realm of the Day. The idea of committed art [*l'art engagé*] seems to him inconsistent for the simple reason that the effect of art in history is quite negligible and the poster, newspaper article and scientific treatise serve history much better than does the poem. But art—differing in this from the World, Mastery and History—is neither the disinterested cult of esthetes, a vision of a world behind the world that blind intellect would fail to recognize, nor the sensible revelation of the concept, which would as such be already past, outdated, in a time when the concept is realized through work. But nothing has been said by placing the work of art outside the Useful, for the question remains: In what does this "sublimation" of the real, which makes it into a work of art, consist? Literature, in Blanchot's view, is foreign to the World and the worlds-behind-the-world; it presupposes the poet's vision, which is an original experience in both senses of the adjective: a fundamental experience, and an experience of the origin. All artistic "disinterestedness" toward things has already been that experience. We do not go from the thing to the poetic image simply by a neutralizing of the real, nor from everyday language to the image of language that constitutes poetic usage, by diminution. According to Blanchot a prior transcendence (though he does not use this term) is required in order for things to be able to be perceived as images, and language as poetry. In this sense, the image precedes perception. What is this transcendent vision?

The much-celebrated "contemplation" does not disenchant the world of things. Whatever is most alien and strange, by virtue of its appearing, already offers *power* a foothold, in subordinating itself to me. The countless worlds conceived by thought, projected by imagination, or divined by instinct, constitute but one world—however *tele*pathic or *meta*physical may be the transcendence of the feeling or knowledge attaining them. Truth, however bold and fresh, leaves us our sovereignty of self and the horizons of the World.

Truth ends up in history, in the solution of all human problems on a human level. Like popular religion, it carries all the earthly forms over into its beyond. It flees life toward life, as in the famous text by Ibn Gabriol, in which man takes shelter from God in God. How to get out of the World? How can the Other (which Jankélévitch calls the *absolutely other* and Blanchot "eternal streaming of the outside") appear, that is, be for someone, without already losing its alterity and exteriority by that way of offering itself to view? How can there be appearing without power?

3 Impersonal Speech and the Presence of Absence

The mode of revelation of what remains *other*, despite its revelation, is not the thought, but the language, of the poem. Its privilege, in Blanchot's analyses, does not consist in leading us

[margin note: Blanchot's "other" + the outside]

further than knowledge. It is not telepathic: the outside is not the distant. It is what appears—but in a singular fashion—when all the real has been denied: realization of that unreality. Its way of being, its nature, consists in being present without being given, in not delivering itself up to the powers, since negation has been the ultimate human power, in being the domain of the impossible, on which power can get no purchase, in being a perpetual dismissal of the one who discloses it. Hence, for one who gazes upon the impossible, an essential solitude, incommensurable with the feeling of isolation and abandonment—haughty or desperate—in the world. A solitude in the desolate field of impossibilities incapable of constituting themselves as worlds.

Literature, says Blanchot, leads to this. It has always given voice to that which was not world—the gods and heroes, when exploits and combat were not Action and Politics but heroism and adventure. Today, now that the gods have left, literature lets speak and be accomplished that which is most radically non-world: the being of beings, the very presence of their disappearance. To show this, Blanchot resumes his earlier meditations on Mallarmé and Kafka. To write is to return to essential language, which consists in moving things aside in words, and echoing being. The being of things is not named in the work of art, but says itself there, coinciding with the absence of things that words are. To be is to speak, but in the absence of any interlocutor. An impersonal speech, without "you," without address, without vocative, and yet distinct from the "coherent discourse" which manifests a Universal Reason belonging to the order of the Day. All works of art are more perfectly works of art to the degree that their authors do not count, as if they served an anonymous order. Kafka really began to write when he replaced "I" with "he," for "the writer belongs to a language no one speaks." Not that a universal and eternal ideal rules writing. Blanchot shows how the impersonality of the work is that of the silence following the departure of the gods, as inextinguishable as a murmur. It is the impersonality of the time into which historical time

[margin note: literature lets speak the ilya]

[margin note: impersonal speech — which is also not discursive — not the dialectic of signification]

(which we, as the children of history, can deny) sinks away; or the impersonality of the night in which the negation of the Day (which we, again, as children of the Day, deny) springs up. The creator is he or she whose name is obliterated and whose memory has faded away. "The creator is without power over his work." To write is to break the bond uniting the word [*parole*] to myself—to invert the relationship that makes me speak to a *thou*—"to echo that which cannot cease speaking." If vision and knowledge consist in *being able* over their objects, in dominating them from a distance, the exceptional reversal brought about by writing comes down to being touched by what one sees—to being touched from a distance. The gaze is seized by the work [*l'œuvre*], the words look at the writer. (This is Blanchot's definition of fascination.) The poetic language that moved the world aside lets the incessant murmur of that distancing reappear, like a night manifesting itself in the night. It is not the impersonal of eternity, but the incessant, the interminable, recommencing below whatever negation of it may be undertaken.

"the words look at the writer."

A situation Blanchot associates with death. To write is to die. To Blanchot, death is not the pathos of the ultimate human possibility, the possibility of impossibility, but the ceaseless repetition of what cannot be grasped, before which the *I* loses its ipseity. The impossibility of possibility. The literary work brings us closer to death, because death is that endless rustle of being that the work causes to murmur. In death as in the work of art, the regular order is reversed, since, in it, power leads to what is unassumable. Thus the distance between life and death is infinite. Also infinite is the poet's work before the inexhaustible language that is the unfolding [*déroulement*] or more precisely the rolling [*roulis*] or even the commotion of being. Death is not the end, it is the never-ending ending. As in certain of Edgar Allan Poe's tales, in which the threat gets closer and closer and the helpless gaze measures that ever still distant approach.

Thus Blanchot determines writing as a quasi-mad structure in the general economy of being, by which being is no longer an economy, as it no longer possesses, when approached through writing, any abode—no longer has any interiority. It is literary space, that is, absolute exteriority: the exteriority of absolute exile. This is what Blanchot also calls the "second night," that which in the first night, which is the normal ending and annihilation of day, becomes presence of that annihilation and thus returns unceasingly to being; a presence Blanchot describes in terms such as lapping [*clapotement*], murmur, dull repetition [*ressassement*]: an entire vocabulary to express the inessential (so to speak) character of that being of the second night. Presence of absence, fullness of emptiness,

> "unfurling" of that which nevertheless hides and remains closed—a light shining on the dark, a light bright from the clarity of this darkness, which abducts and ravishes the dark in the first light of the unfurling, but also disappears into the absolutely obscure whose essence is to close in upon whatever would reveal it, to attract this disclosure into itself and swallow it up.[7]

Writing would be the unlikely procedure of a power that, at a moment called inspiration, "swerves" into non-power. It would be the very rhythm of being, so that literature would have no object but itself. (And someday the latent meaning of Blanchot's novelistic work will have to be articulated.) Modern art speaks of nothing but the adventure of art itself; it strives to be pure painting, pure music. No doubt the critical and philosophical work, relating that adventure, is far below art, which is the voyage into the end of the night itself, and not merely the travel narrative. And yet Blanchot's research brings to the philosopher a "category" and a new "way of knowing" that I would like to clarify, independently of the philosophy of art proper.

4 The Errancy of Being

The essence of art, from this perspective, is the passage from language to the ineffable that says itself, the making visible of the obscurity of the elemental through the work. To describe the work in this way, filled with contradictions, is not dialectic, because no level of thought emerges at which that alternance is overcome, at which contradiction is reconciled. If thought did achieve this level, rising up to the synthesis, we would still remain in the world, on the terrain of human possibilities and initiatives, in Action and the Meaningful. Thus literature casts us upon a shore where no thought can land—it lets out onto the unthinkable. Only here does the idealist metaphysics of the *esse-percipi* come to an end. Literature is the unique adventure of a transcendence beyond all the horizons of the world, which even the boldest departures do not let us flee. Only art would let us "take off"—but for the fact that in that conquest of exteriority, we must remain for ever excluded; for, if it did offer shelter to the poet, exteriority would have lost its very strangeness. That unthinkable, to which the poem (i.e. the work) leads without leading there—Blanchot calls it being. Already in Heidegger, art, beyond all esthetic meaning, made the "truth of being" shine forth, but it shared that ability with other forms of existence. Blanchot sees art's vocation as exclusive. But above all, writing does not lead to the truth of being. One might say that it leads to the errancy of being—to being as a place of going astray, to the uninhabitable. Thus one would be equally justified in saying that literature does not lead there, since it is impossible to reach a destination. The errancy of being—more external than truth. In Heidegger, an alternance of nothingness and being also occurs in the truth of being; but Blanchot, contrary to Heidegger, does not call it truth, but non-truth. He insists on this veil of the "no," this inessential character of the ultimate essence of the work. This *no* is unlike the Hegelian and Marxist negativity: the labor that changes nature, the political activity that changes society. Being, revealed by the work—brought to self-expression—is beyond all possibility, like death, which one cannot assume despite the eloquence of suicide, for *I* never die, *one* always dies; though this is not, as Heidegger thinks, because of flight before the responsibility for one's own death. And yet it is in this non-true to which literature leads, and not in the "truth of being,"

that authenticity resides. Authenticity that is not truth: this is
perhaps the ultimate proposition to which Blanchot's critical
reflection leads us. And I think it is an invitation to leave the
Heideggerian world.

5 The Call to Errancy

The non-true as the essential form of authenticity. That con-
clusion is formulated in the form of a question. And "at a level
closer to historical actuality" a footnote on page 260 explains it.

> [O]ne might say: the more the world is affirmed as the future and
> the broad daylight of truth, where everything will have value, bear
> meaning, where the whole will be achieved under the mastery of
> man and for his use, the more it seems that art must descend toward
> that point where nothing has meaning yet, the more it matters that
> art maintain the movement, the insecurity and the grief of that
> which escapes every grasp and all ends. The artist and the poet seem
> to have received this mission: to call us obstinately back to error, to
> turn us toward that space where everything we propose, everything
> we have acquired, everything we are, all that is disclosed on earth
> [and in heaven], returns to insignificance, and where what
> approaches is the nonserious and the nontrue, as if perhaps thence
> sprang the source of all authenticity.[8]

To call us back to error: this cannot mean a nihilistic or
diabolical substitution of falsehood for truth. Nor do these lines
in any way suggest a romanticism of the fortunate error, spurring
us on to movement and life. Here the thought is more disillusioned, more mature. It is even further removed from the eternal
illusion that desperately flees the absurdity of being: the opium
that Malraux, in *Man's Fate*, elevates to the rank of category,
opposing and juxtaposing it to the difficult task of Revolution.
The Day, the Meaningful, the World, Human Control—all that
must come. But the ultimate meaning to be taken on by this
Day, this place, this World produced by work and history must
be decided upon. And it may be that here Blanchot and

Heidegger stand in radical opposition—after so many points of perfect agreement.

Heidegger's late philosophy consists predominantly in the interpretation of the essential forms of human activity—art, technology, science, economy—as modes of truth (or the forgetting of it). The fact that, for Heidegger, the approach to that truth, the response to that call, is made by wandering byways, and that error is contemporaneous with truth—the fact that the revelation of being is also its dissimulation: all this shows a very high degree of proximity between Heidegger's notion of being and that realization of unreality, that presence of absence, that existence of nothingness that, according to Blanchot, the work of art, the poem, allows us to express. But in Heidegger's view truth—a primordial disclosure—conditions all wanderings, and that is why all that is human can be said, in the final analysis, in terms of truth—be described as "disclosure of being." In Blanchot, *the work uncovers, in an uncovering that is not truth,* a darkness. In an uncovering that is not truth! That is an odd way of uncovering and seeing the "content" determined by its formal structure: a darkness absolutely external, on which no hold is possible. As in a desert, one can find no place to reside. From the depths of sedentary existence a nomadic memory arises. Nomadism is not an approach to the sedentary state. It is an irreducible relation to the earth: a sojourn devoid of *place*. Before the darkness to which art recalls us, as before death, the "I," mainstay of our powers, dissolves into an anonymous "one" in a land of peregrination. It is the *I* of the Eternal Wanderer, identified by gait rather than location, along the border of non-truth, a realm extending farther than the true. Truth conditioned by errancy, errancy conditioned by truth: a distinction without a difference? I think not.

6 The Authenticity of Exile

The orthodox Heideggerians admit of no other discriminating features between two thoughts than those involving the truth of being that governs them. But that *modus operandi* presupposes the primacy of the truth of being, which is still in question here. They have nothing but disdain for any reference to ethical certainties, which would indicate an inferior thinking, an insufficient thinking—opinion. The appeal to ethics runs contrary to the fundamental dogma of Heideggerian orthodoxy: priority of being [*être*] in relation to beings [*l'étant*]. Yet ethics does not replace truth with falsehood, but situates man's first breath not in the light of being but in the relation to a being, prior to the thematization of that being. Such a relation, in which the being [*étant*] does not become my object, is precisely justice.

The literary space into which Blanchot (who also abstains from ethical preoccupations, at least in explicit form) leads us has nothing in common with the Heideggerian world that art renders inhabitable. Art, according to Blanchot, far from elucidating the world, exposes the desolate, lightless substratum underlying it, and restores to our sojourn its exotic essence—and, to the wonders of our architecture, their function of makeshift desert shelters. Blanchot and Heidegger agree that art does not lead (contrary to classical esthetics) to a world behind the world, an ideal world behind the real one. Art is light. Light from on high in Heidegger, making the world, founding place. In Blanchot it is a black light, a night coming from below—a light that undoes the world, leading it back to its origin, to the over and over again, the murmur, ceaseless lapping of waves, a "deep past, never long enough ago."[9] The poetic quest for the unreal is the quest for the deepest recess of that real.

Makeshift desert shelters. Our concern here is not with going back in history. But for Blanchot, literature recalls the human essence of nomadism. Is nomadism not the source of a meaning, appearing in a light cast by no marble, but by the face of man? If the authenticity Blanchot speaks of is to mean anything other than a consciousness of the lack of seriousness of edification, anything other than derision—the authenticity of art must herald an order of justice, the slave morality that is absent from the Heideggerian city. Does man as *a being*, as this man standing before me, exposed to hunger, thirst and cold, truly accomplish, in his needs, the disclosure of being? Has he already, as such, been the vigilant guardian of the light? Heidegger's world is a world of lords who have transcended the condition of needy, wretched human beings, or a world of servants whose only concern is for these lords. Action, there, is heroism; dwelling, the prince's palace and the temple of the gods, which are seen as part of the landscape before being places of shelter. A life of mortals consoled by the visit of gods and their magnificence. A life of toil upon ancestral soil that no upheaval could ever take away. It is that calm possession, that pagan enrootedness that characterizes all Heidegger's mention of things—whether it be of a bridge, or a pitcher, or a pair of shoes. Let us recall those dazzling analyses of dwelling and of the thing in his last publication.[10] The reference to sky and earth, mortals and gods (always in the plural)—to their fourfoldness, indissoluble in the place and the object, assures an absoluteness of perception, of the place in which the world and geometric space itself, and the sky and the earth as simply determinants of space, are situated. That primacy, that absoluteness of the landscape in which the relation to man is not separate from the three other relations, certainly flatters our taste as privileged persons and as Europeans. But it implies asserting the impossibility of human wretchedness. The idealism of the haughty! Can we be sure that perception is transcended only by mathematical abstractions—and fallaciously so, since abstractions spring from a place, and no place can be harbored in a geometrical space?[11] Was not perception—long before the gods, landscapes, and Greek or German mathematicians —abandoned as a system of reference in the revelation of the Invisible God which "no sky can contain"? The God of justice, of the desert and of men. At stake here was—before the stories that religions tell children and women—a new dimension of Height and Ideal. Surely Heidegger knows this. But while the Hellenic "truth of being" merits a subtle hermeneutics, the monotheist revelation is always expedited in a few unnuanced theological formulas. In the accursed cities where dwelling is stripped of its architectural wonders, not only are the gods absent, but the sky itself. But in monosyllabic hunger, in the wretched poverty in which houses and objects revert to their material function and enjoyment is closed in on all sides, the face of man shines forth. Does Blanchot not attribute to art the function of uprooting the Heideggerian universe? Does not the poet, before the "eternal streaming of the outside," hear the voices that call away from the Heideggerian world? A world that is not frightening because of its nihilism. It is not nihilistic. But, in it, justice does not condition truth—it remains for ever closed to certain texts, a score of centuries old, in which Amalek's existence prevents the integrity of the Divine Name—that is, precisely, the *truth of being*.

2 The Servant and Her Master

(1966)

I

Artistic activity makes the artist aware that he is not the author of his works. Efficient causality, in daily activities, links the worker unambiguously to his product—at the same time making it possible to assess the respective roles of the matter used, the goal pursued and the formal and legal necessities of the enterprise undertaken. But in the case of the artist, efficient causality is at the service of a summons penetrating it through and through. It is subjected to mysterious voices, mysterious because not comparable with the voice heard in a normal collaboration. It is consumed by calls that curve the very rectilinearity of its propulsion.

This awareness of a foreign interference in human causality, this age-old experience of inspiration (upon which *L'attente L'oubli*[1] opens, perhaps), an experience to which the artist joyfully surrenders and which so many present-day optimistic philosophies of art acclaim as a surpassing of self (though Valéry felt humiliated by it), takes on an exceptional gravity in light of the following questions. Do not enthusiasm or possession lurk hidden in the depths of all activity, including the primordial activity of consciousness and language? Is thought not borne by a delirium deeper than itself? Is not language—which claims to be act and origin, the decisive word, and the possibility, if ever there was one, of finishing, of breaking off—an inveterate passivity, the repetition of an old story without beginning or end, an impersonal and deep stirring that sensation only washes over with a surface ripple?

The disrepute into which the supernatural has fallen in the thought and mores of the West has not affected the mystery of inspiration. Not so long ago, one still distinguished, in poetic prôduction, the part of the intellect, master of its intentions, belonging to the thinker in control of his or her thoughts, of no interest perhaps, but inalienable; and the best part, that of genius, the demon, the muse, the unconscious. Surrealism, despite its daring, still belonged to that stage, in its theory of automatic writing which had to be freed from conscious thought. But it thus admitted that inspiration has a powerful rival that had to be put to sleep in advance. In Blanchot's *Aminadab*, Thomas is chained to a companion whose prisoner he is, or who is his. And thus, in *L'attente L'oubli*: "He began to hear, to one side of what she said, and, as it were, in the background ... other words with which hers had almost nothing in common" (25)[2]. As if persons, by dint of being identical, became double—as if consciousness, despite its freedom, fulfilled a function it had never assumed.

"But everything remains unchanged" (29). The other is but a repetition of the same, and the other speech echoes the first, despite its difference. Absurdity at the heart of absurdity: the alienation of consciousness does not free it from itself. Nothing *extra*-ordinary takes place. Language is obliged to continue under the original conditions in which it began. Its movement toward the outside is forever paralyzed by the commitments that those first words implied, and that each new word tacitly brings back. The idea that God has withdrawn from the world, or that God is dead, may be the expression of that monotony, multiplying and spreading out in infinite variations, and of the *I*, incapable of remaining quietly within its identity. "It is endlessly restless" (40). Blanchot's work attempts to untie the double knot of non-sense, that monstrosity, previously inexpressed, of the identical, which begins proliferating like a cancerous cell, without producing anything other than repetition and tautology. "Is there still the same light, even though it is night" (35)?

The destiny of our world, which has lost the ability to speak, is at stake in this work. "Make it possible for me to speak to you": such is the invocation dominating the entire first part of *L'attente L'oubli*. One can no longer speak, not only because of that alien admixture, but also because of the tautological rhythm that runs through the dialogue itself—because of the droning that immediately closes the openings of communication. As if everything were, since time immemorial, over. To speak, to write, is to try to break open the definitiveness of eternity; but does discourse have the last word? Does that not belong to the ontological act that this discourse accomplishes, and that already immures this discourse? Words change into being, which does not signify by its discursive intention. "She spoke truly, but not in what she said" (36). "They would always converse there," says another crucial text, "of the instant when they would no longer be there. Even though they knew they would always be there talking about such an instant, they thought there was nothing more worthy of their eternity than to spend it evoking its end" (35). Can one get out of this circle otherwise than by expressing the impossibility of getting out—than by saying the inexpressible? Is not poetry, of itself, the way out? Blanchot would therefore oppose Hegel's doctrine that art has been dead since the end of antiquity, that it was subordinated to religion during the Middle Ages, and to philosophy in our time. This is not, of course, some noble revolt against the prose of the technological age. It is a daring thought. Blanchot challenges the apparently unquestionable claim of a certain language to be the privileged conveyer of the meaningful—to be its beginning, its middle and its end. Does the meaningful depend upon a certain order of propositions built upon a certain grammar in order for it to constitute a logical discourse? Or does meaning make language explode, and then mean among these broken bits (grammar, in

Blanchot, comes out safe and sound!), but already in spirit and in truth without awaiting any later interpretation? *L'attente L'oubli* denies the philosophical language of interpretation, which "speaks incessantly" (and to which Blanchot, as literary critic, conforms), the dignity of being an ultimate language. To seek—beyond the poetic discourse that expresses, dispersedly, the impossible escape from discourse—the logos that gathers, is to block the opening through which the circularity of coherent discourse announces (but also denounces, and in so doing transcends) itself. Could one not then venture further, and think that the presuppositions of coherent speech can no longer refute what speech wants to say? And perhaps we are wrong in using the designation art and poetry for that exceptional event, that sovereign forgetting, that liberates language from its servitude with respect to the structures in which the *said* maintains itself. Perhaps Hegel was right as far as art is concerned. What counts—whether it be called poetry or what you will—is that a meaning is able to proffer itself beyond the closed discourse of Hegel; that a meaning that forgets the presuppositions of that discourse becomes *fable*.

II

Blanchot's properly literary work brings us primarily a new feeling: a new "experience," or, more precisely, a new prickling sensation of the skin, brushed against by things. It all begins at this tangible level: these places—the hotel rooms, the kitchen, the hallways, the windows, the walls—in which space weighs by its very transparency, "exerting the same constant pressure in not exerting it" (31); the resonance that dies down through that space and does not cease dying down at the edge of a silence from which it issues like a distant purring with which silence is merged at first: "in place of the beginning a sort of initial void, an energetic refusal to let the story begin" (22); the remoteness and strangeness of things heavy with their meaninglessness: a glass of water, a bed, a table, an armchair—expelled, abstract;

the transparency of a dialogue between the initiates, reduced to the verbal markers between which an unspoken understanding—without mystery for the interlocutors, but opaque with its own emptiness—slides by. Always that inverted conversation of erosion—which takes place where there is in fact nothing. "Innumerable peopling of the void" (54), like the rising of an obtuse suffering, the secret, slow tumefaction of Nothingness. The effort of nothingness and, as it were, the way it labors, strains and "happens" and steps aside from its identity of emptiness, "the voices echo in the immense void, the emptiness of voices and the void of these empty places" (18–19). The silence that sets in does not stop the droning sound. It is already here from the other side of the wall, and no negation can silence this commotion: isn't the other noise the same as the one that was just reduced to silence, on this side? Was it in order to hear it that they tried to keep quiet? Was it to hear "the same word coming back toward itself" (38–39) that they tried to speak? "The old words that want to be there again without speaking … a rumor without a trace … nowhere wandering, everywhere dwelling" (13). "Again, again walking and always in the same place—another country, other towns, the same country" (14). Language is closed, like that room. "How they suffocated together in that closed place, in which the words they spoke to one another could no longer mean anything but that closure. Didn't she keep saying just: 'We are locked in, we will never get out of here'" (28–29)? The words follow one another, interrupting the ones that preceded them. *They never leave off leaving.* "Poor room … how little I live in you. Aren't I just staying in it to get rid of all the traces of my stay" (13–14)? An eternal present; the eternity of the tautology or iteration.

III

"Is there a door he hasn't noticed? Is there a bare wall there by two window openings?" (35). Is it possible to get out, or on the contrary is even the light that seems to illuminate this sojourn artificial, and does one's consciousness of the situation get lost in the same endless game that language plays, without reaching any *cogito*? Poetic language will make a breach in the wall, protecting itself from the rubble of that breakthrough, which threatens to bury and immobilize the forward movement by breaking it down into projects and memories—synchronic and eternally contemporary in meaning. The game that consists in staying in a place to remove the traces of one's stay must not recommence. She struggled, Blanchot says, "against certain words that had been, as it were, deposited in her, and that she strove to keep connected with the future or with something that hadn't happened yet, though already present, though already past" (17). It is perhaps this movement—which undoes words, reducing them to the present—that Blanchot calls Waiting, Forgetting [*L'attente L'oubli*].

the Event

not (?)

Forgetting opposed to remembering, waiting that is not a waiting for something. "Waiting, waiting that is the refusal to wait for anything, a calm expanse, disclosed step by step" (20). Waiting, Forgetting, juxtaposed, without any conjunction having linked them in a structure. They do not designate states of the soul, whose intentionality, with its countless threads, would further consolidate the inextricable weave of being, turning back and closing itself on itself. Subjectivity knots and reinforces the fabric of the world: someone in the fabric of being makes a niche for himself, "feathers his nest." Waiting, Forgetting, loosen that ontological field, release a thread, untie, erode, relax, obliterate. "An initial distraction" (20)! The instant, "laden with its entire past and big with its future," the instant of the present whose tensed dynamism makes everything contemporary and eternal, returns to tranquility in waiting. Neither foresight nor impatience, "waiting awaits nothing" (51). And forgetting turns away from the past instant but keeps a relationship with what it turns away from "when it remains in words" (69). Here diachrony is restored to time. A nocturnal time: "the night in which nothing is awaited represents this movement of waiting" (50). But the primordial forgetting is the forgetting of oneself. Is not *ipseity*, at the same time as being absolute origin, the insatiable turning back to self, the imprisonment of self by self, which language also is? Reflection brings up the old foundation stones and mixes them with current things. That simultaneity of conditioning and conditioned is known as coherent discourse. But, looking back to examine their condition, words are immobilized, become pillars of salt. Here, again, Forgetting restores diachrony to time. A diachrony with neither pretention nor retention. To await nothing and forget everything—the opposite of subjectivity—"absence of any center" (45). A relaxing of the *I*—of its tensing upon itself—of that "existence for which, in its existence, it is a question of that very existence."[3] "With what melancholy, but what calm certainty, he felt he could never again say *I*" (34). "She detached him from himself" (44). The interlocutors, in the second part of the book, so calm, often light-hearted and triumphant, instead of being tensed upon themselves, renounce their identity without losing it, let go of themselves like butterflies letting go of their chrysalises, as if extricating themselves from a garment and immediately regaining their composure; move toward the Other, abandon themselves, rejoin themselves stripped of self and present to self (how many new relations between self and self!), find a door, in this relaxed self, beyond being, and, in an expression that combines equality, justice, caress, communication and transcendence—an admirable expression by its accuracy and gracefulness—"are together, but not yet" (76).

IV

That poetic word, for Blanchot, becomes a word that contradicts itself. The beauty (an almost tangible beauty) of that contradictory alternation of verbal exchanges in his works, and especially in *L'attente L'oubli*, is well known. The affirmation is followed, often in the same proposition, by its negation. Saying lets go of what it grasps. The thing that is given—being—does not measure up to Waiting and its hyperbolic intention beyond

Being, whereas subjectivity asks only to be absorbed in the object that "the intentionality of consciousness" holds within its reach. Saying is Desire that the approach of the Desirable exacerbates, deepens, and therefore in which the approach of the Desirable becomes more distant. Such is the scintillating modality of transcendence—of that which truly *comes to pass*.[4]

A discontinuous and contradictory language of scintillation. A language that, beyond meanings, can make a sign to us. The sign is made from afar, from the beyond, and beyond. Poetic language signals to us, without the sign's bearing a meaning by giving up meaning. But it is absolutely "in clear,"[5] on the hither side and beyond the inevitable conventions of languages. Though outside the coded system of languages, it leads to it, in the manner of the meta-language mentioned in logistics,[6] which "unlocks" the symbolism of writing.

To give a sign, without its standing for anything. Blanchot speaks admirably of it. "It is the voice that was confided, and not what it said. What it said, the secrets you gather and transcribe to highlight them—you must gently draw them back, despite their temptation of seduction, toward the silence you first drew from them" (11). Poetry, in Blanchot's view, transforms words—indices of a manifold, moments of a totality—into signs set free, that break through the walls of immanence, disrupting order. Two beings locked in a room struggle with a fatality that brings them too close together or sets them too far apart (42) to find a door. No novel, no poem—from the *Iliad* to *Remembrance of Things Past*—has done anything other than this. To introduce a meaning into Being is to move from Same to the Other, from *I* to the other person; it is to give a sign, to undo the structures of language. Without that, the world would know nothing but the meanings that inform the minutes or reports of corporate board meetings.

V

The fact that the poetic verb can nevertheless betray itself— that it can become swallowed up by the order, appear as a

a "language of
pure transcendence"

cultural product, a document or testimony, be encouraged,
applauded and highly prized, sold, bought, consumed—the fact
that it can be consoling, speak alone in the language of a
people—this can be explained by the very place in which it
springs up (and there is no other): between the knowledge that
encompasses the Whole, and the culture into which it blends,
two jaws that threaten to close down upon it. Blanchot seeks
precisely the moment, between seeing and saying, at which the
jaws are not quite closed.

Between seeing and saying. Already the order that is eternally
present to vision has been abandoned. But still there are signs,
"words that evoke nothing" (19), still on the hither side of the
cultural and historical order. The latter has already jolted the
simultaneity of the vision of its completed world and pulled it
into history. Still, it will become fixed in the form of a story,
enveloped in the totality of the *said*, which totality will alone
confer a meaning upon what is said—even if each discourse were
to produce, in its own way, that clarifying totality, and have its
own way of pushing on to the end. "No one here wants to be
tied to a story" (22). "Make it impossible for me to talk to you"
is a prayer, as is "Make it possible for me to talk to you." It
preserves that movement that is located between seeing and saying,
that language of pure transcendence without correlation—like
the waiting that nothing awaited yet destroys—noesis without
noema—pure extra-vagance, a language going from one singularity to another without their having anything in common
("There is still too much in common between the interlocutors,"
it says on page 64), a language without words that beckons
before signifying anything, a language of pure complicity, but of
a purposeless complicity: "She gave the impression, when she
spoke, of not knowing how to tie the words to the wealth of a
prior language. They were without history, without any link
with the collective past; even without any connection with her
own life, anyone else's" (24). Is this the language, stronger than
prayer and battle, to which Lermontov responds in the mysterious
poem here translated (in bad prose)?

There are utterances—their meaning/is obscure or negligible—/but without emotion/one cannot understand them./ How full their sounds are/of the madness of desire!/ In them the tears of separation/in them the trembling of reunion./ No response/in the noise of the world/to the verb that was born/of flame and light./ But in the temple, in battle/and wherever I may be/as soon as I hear it/I will recognize it everywhere/ Without finishing the prayer/ I will answer it/And out of the battle/ I will rush to meet it.

But the language that beckons without taking its place within the eternity of the signified idea—the discontinuous language—is circumvented by the ancillary word that follows its traces and does not cease talking. The coherent word in which being (and even "the Being of beings") stretches out is all memory, all foresight, all eternity. Inexhaustible, it gets the last word. It contaminates with logic the equivocal that is inscribed in the trace of forgotten discourse, and it never indulges in enigma. How can we order one who speaks the truth to be silent? It is like a servant who puts a plausible face on the extravagant behavior of her master, and who has a reputation for loving wisdom. She derives victory and presence from narrating the failures, absences and escapades of him whom she serves and spies on. She knows exactly what is contained in the hiding-places she cannot open, and keeps the keys to doors that have been destroyed. A housekeeper beyond reproach, she keeps careful check on the house she rules over, and disputes the existence of secret locks.

Housekeeper or mistress? Marvelous hypocrite! For she loves the madness she keeps watch over.

3 A Conversation with André Dalmas

André Dalmas.-*What we notice from the outset in Françoise Collin's study[1] is not just its philosophical approach to M. Blanchot's work, which, you will agree, is fully justified. This book lets you hear, from the depths, a frankly moving echo, revealing the reader's adventure—that waiting, filled with something that does not appear. Not the fear of saying too much; rather that of not saying enough—though everything cannot be said. Aren't we dealing with a more general problem—the crisis of philosophical language?*

Emmanuel Levinas.—The project of our conversation dates from long before the publication of Françoise Collin's book. I was not notified in advance of the homage with which I find myself associated at the beginning of the work. But you know how highly I thought of this text long before it was printed. I am not going to cancel our project. Françoise Collin's effort and success in this book (the first, as you say, devoted to Blanchot) do, in fact, seem remarkable to me. And all I may say to you is based on the virtualities emerging from her vigorous and nuanced interpretation.

To bring Blanchot's work into a philosophical discourse is to shed light on it as much by what one says about it as by what one cannot say. This unsaid has nothing in common with Heidegger's famous "unsaid," which authorizes our understanding Kant or Hegel better than they understood themselves. You know how much that notion is misused these days. The literary exercise in which Blanchot speaks is an exercise of writing whose break with order—with gathering together, the collection of terms, their synchrony, the logos—is clearly shown by Françoise Collin.

Literature does not express that dispersion: it is its event. ★ With a rare gift for hearing the concordance of those texts in which that bursting forth (or that dissemination) takes place, and fully aware that she is embarking on an enterprise that is against nature, Françoise Collin, in bringing out Blanchot's main tenets, leaves literature in its unenglobable space, as if it were isolating itself from any philosophy. The significance Blanchot attributes to literature challenges the arrogance of philosophical discourse—that englobing discourse, capable of saying everything, *including its own failure.*

A dissemination of that which used to gather together into a logos! Saying is here reduced to unsaying itself, retracting, backtracking, when it declares literature to be this or that. The extraordinary aspect of literature—neither being nor non-being—imposes itself without imposing itself: The Neuter, the Savage, the Stranger, Negation of the Order, "A departure from Numbers and of Beings,"[2] to use Baudelaire's terms, and yet an incessant commotion, a silence that resonates without any possible interruption, beyond all sonority. Writing means to be done with all that, and is never done being done, in opening up the unenglobable literary space.

It is also a challenging of philosophy that is not a challenging. For challenging in this case does not entail any claim to englobe: the englobing tendency is philosophical, and would reintegrate "literary space" into the space of the world. It is impossible to annex this excluded middle, of which literature would be the incredible modulation. It is absolutely set apart. Françoise Collin shows us that Blanchot does not bring us a "singular notion," derived from a meditation on literature. It is because an "un-essence" of that order (or that "extra-ordinary") besieges being that literature "excuses." Into the Trojan Horse of the *cultural product*, which belongs to the Order, this "chaos" is inserted that rocks all the thinkable.

André Dalmas-*For M. Blanchot, the writer's adventure is the trying experience of the dispossession of the self. We know this today. Françoise Collin draws our attention to that phrase from* Thomas the Obscure,[3] *"I think, therefore I am not," which could be interpreted as "I speak, therefore I am not." Traditional literature would be the compromise by which the writer, drawn out of himself, saves what can be saved of his relations with the world and himself, a way of defending himself from this return toward anonymity, toward what M. Blanchot calls the Neuter. Is this Neuter present or absent? Is it manifested in writing by pure affirmation, or negation?*

Emmanuel Levinas.—This Neuter, or this Excluded Middle, is neither affirmation nor pure negation of being. For affirmation and negation are in the Order, they are part of it. And yet the insistence of this Neuter bears an exclusively negative quality. One does not mix [*fraye*] with it—it is the "frightening" ["*l'effrayant*"] *par excellence*. And all the novelistic portion of Blanchot's work bathes in that atmosphere of a reality of the unreal—a presence of absence that is heavy, like the atmosphere after death into which Blanchot has brought us since *Thomas the Obscure* (first version). Perhaps the ambiguity of this Neuter is manifested in the brisk liveliness and ease recovered by the stiff movements of characters unable to cross a room or hallway.

The presence of absence is not pure negation. Does not writing become poetry? The anonymous and incessant droning—is it not overcome by song filling the literary space? So it is in *L'attente L'oubli*,[4] in which, in an interminable hesitation, the language is at once affirmative and negative—but the narrative ends on cheerful, almost exultant pages.

André Dalmas.-*That after-death atmosphere is often mentioned by Françoise Collin. Is that the domain of this so frightening and new Neuter? I say "so new," because this Neuter seems to me radically different from Heidegger's, which is above man, commands thought and renders it intelligible.*

[Handwritten note, top left margin: Blanchot's Neuter as transcendence — see esp. p. 155 ✱]

[Handwritten note, right margin: the Neuter: beyond Being]

Emmanuel Levinas.—Blanchot's Neuter, an after-death distance "with respect to being" that is not achieved by simple negation, is foreign to the world—with a foreignness beyond all foreignness: exponentially foreign, so to speak. Further away than any God. Totally otherwise than the *Sein* [to be]—which is also anonymous—of Heidegger, which (differing from the Existent, as you rightly point out), is the luminosity of the world itself—locale, countryside, peace. It requires Blanchot's entire novelistic works, and all the art of his own saying in his theoretical works, to suggest an absolute remoteness (or an exit) from the World, a reversal of the ontological categories—achieved here in a breathlessness of spirit. This work, an exacerbation of alterity, impugns the traditional transcendence that, ever recuperable, insures a world even more sure of itself than the world without God.

One is even astonished when Françoise Collin speaks of "the experience of literature," as if it could be a question of a discovery or an experience, where literally, for Blanchot, there is nothing left. Unless it be the void of absence itself and the long gaping of its abyss.

Thought, on the basis of knowledge that proceeds from the given and attaches itself to the intuitive, can *think* the meaning of what it cannot see (Kant), or else place all knowledge in the thought of the invisible, which remains determinable and determined (Hegel). Beyond that limit, there is, according to Blanchot, in a non-place, something that cannot be thought, and that does not knock at thought's door—a something that is not a something, but that writing wants to drown out—a purely verbal adventure if there ever was one. ... The whole of literature, in this view, does its utmost to cross out its meaning by crossing out the crossing-out, and the crossings-out of the crossings-out. And so on ... infinitely. This is a position of the writer that goes against nature, an interminable retroactivity of one who erases his traces, and the traces of the erasure of the traces. In the image (but in reverse) of a fire that consumes a bush that it does not succeed in consuming,[5] as if feeding on its own heat.

André Dalmas.-*One of the lessons (and not the least) that Françoise Collin draws from her reading of Blanchot is the irreducibility of writing to discourse. She writes that "what appears in writing appears in writing only, and does not have the power of a truth that would subsist outside it." If I understand that correctly, writing does not destroy: it disrupts, shakes and disperses the* said, *causing something that cannot keep silent to appear (or be heard)?*

Emmanuel Levinas.—I think Maurice Blanchot's work and thought can be interpreted in two directions at the same time.

On one hand, it is the announcement of a loss of meaning, a scattering of discourse, as if one were at the extreme pinnacle of nihilism—as if nothingness itself could no longer be thought peacefully, and had become equivocal to the ear listening to it. Meaning, bound to language, in becoming literature, in which it should be fulfilled and exalted, brings us back to meaningless repetition—more devoid of meaning than the wandering structures or piecemeal elements that might make it up. We are delivered up to the inhuman, to the frightfulness of the Neuter. That is one direction.

But, on the other hand, here is the world from which Blanchot's literary space is excluded: a world no human suffering keeps from being in order; a world that goes on willy-nilly (What matter? It does not hinder Knowledge—it makes possible a Knowledge liberated from all ideology); a world that constitutes a totality in its indifference to values (good and evil being of equal worth); a world that makes up a whole in the "everything is permitted"of Dostoevsky, not because of his atheism, but because of his spirituality. In truth, nothing is better arranged into its synchronic and even identical totality than such a world—the interiorization of all laws having caused it to lose Difference, and all words having become synonymous, as Jean Paulhan[6] feared. Nothing is more self-sufficient.

Blanchot reminds that world that its totality is not total—that the coherent discourse it vaunts does not catch up with another discourse which it fails to silence. That other discourse is troubled by an uninterrupted noise. A difference does not let the world sleep, and troubles the order in which being and non-being are ordered in a dialectic. This Neuter is not a someone, nor even a something. It is but an *excluded middle* that, properly speaking, *is* not even. Yet there is in it more transcendence than any world-behind-the-worlds[7] ever gave a glimpse of.

4 Exercises on "The Madness of the Day"[1]

1 From Poetry to Prose

The fact that expression is not something added onto thought—that, as metaphor,[2] it carries the thought beyond the theme thought—that beyond this theme, letters (in their unfolding, their literature) are further transmissible, in the manner of a hammer or a document, and retain the seminal reasons of the Said, promising the interpreter, i.e. the reader, a more distant and older or deeper meaning: this is, no doubt, Intelligibility itself. Of itself, and not just for a finite mind, it requires writers and readers. Of itself it requires the Book.

The reading, or the interpretation, can be carried out in a variety of ways. It is each person's role, in the epiphany of Reason which needs each one of us. No reading dispels the multivocal secret or enigma of the true book; but in every reading, beyond the virtualities contained in a writer's project, the countless and future (or ancient) lives of the Written germinate. This obtains even if the writer, intelligent through and through, examines, as reader, his own spontaneity, and already inflects his writing to the sense thereby surprised; writing that need not be automatic to be inspired.

The reading proposed here of a short and no longer recent text of Blanchot's touches upon a few points of its texture as if they had been singled out solely for their symbolic power. A hesitant pedantry? Lese-poetry? Indeed so, but it is also one of the possible lives of that work, even if you reject the idea behind my deciphering: the idea that the irreducible (inspired) exoticism[3] of poetry refers back to [*en appelle à*] a saying *properly so-called*, a saying that thematizes, even if it may be obliged to unsay itself in order to avoid disfiguring the secret it exposes.[4]

It is not easy to speak of Blanchot. The best pages that have been devoted to him in recent years have fortunately abstained—as I shall—from claiming to understand a contemporary and a Blanchot "better than he understood himself." Françoise Collin has established, within Blanchot's literary space, which extends beyond his critical essays, a few useful points of repair, borrowed from contemporary philosophy, and Philippe Boyer has allowed us to hear the echoes of his silence, so to speak, through the noise of current writing.[5] Roger Laporte, in a brilliant and sympathetic text, gives an overview of the entire *œuvre*, and in a manner that is quite personal to him speaks of Blanchot in relating the impossibility of speaking of Blanchot. Bernard Noël encounters Blanchot's *Arrêt de mort* [Death Sentence] in his own life, as if encountering a monster who strikes him almost fatally. A teratomorphy that is probably the modality through which, in the evolution of animal life, mutations appear that lead to the constitution of new species, including man.[6] And Pierre Madaule brings Blanchot's poetic work into the fable of his own poetry.[7] No one has tried to approach Blanchot's text to interrogate its figures indiscreetly, as if a code were applicable to them by which their poetry could be translated into prose. All back away from such presumption, such profanation or treason. But can we be certain (in this case of an art shaping the matter of language) that such an approach, despite all the risks involved, is not the preparatory exercise necessary to all other access? This messy job could be forgotten afterward, once it has made possible the approach to that writing in its significance without signifiers—that is, in its musicality. The difficulty of such a task would alone suffice to explain my choice of a short text. But it, like Blanchot's entire work, probably, is a "fable" about the *closure of being*, which, of its own accord, forms the human: strangulation, but in endless agony. In order to treat the poetry of works as complex as, for example, *Amina-dab* or *Le Très Haut* [The Most High], considerable, perhaps inordinate, intellectual resources would be needed. Whatever may be the extent of those available to the present writer, the irresistible temptation of commentary attests to the fact that for the reader this text on *closure* is inspired—that in it the *other* of the Image and the Letter rend the *same* of the Said, according to a modality of awakening and sobering up [*dégrisement*]—and that this writing is Book.

To that extent the commentary already diverges from it, and finds breathing room in the difference that, at times, separates he who comments upon the Book from the Writer.

2 On Hell

Despite the apparent heterogeneity of its themes, the arrangement or juxtaposition of which would be worthy of special analysis, and apart from its own rhythms and musical effect, the *Madness of the Day* has, as it were, an optical focus. It is its title itself: Madness of the Day. Madness of today, but madness of the day also in the sense that, in it, day is madly desired, and in the sense that day—clarity and measure—goes mad there, and, hence, especially, in the sense that the madness of day is contrasted with the madness or panic of night—with the "dread of the night" of the Song of Songs (3:8), which envelops King Solomon, the prince of peace, despite his splendor.

Madness of today. Not that we are dealing with some "mal du siècle."[8] These twenty-five pages, written shortly after the Liberation (in 1948 or thereabouts) do not bear the signs of the times in which they were written. The allusion to "the madness of the world," and to the return of the world to its equilibrium, says almost nothing of the "psychological and moral" climate of the years Europe had just experienced. One finds even less of the hopes and fears of life just after the war. These pages do not even reflect what was going on in 1948 on the level of the history of ideas. (In this respect, *The Madness of the Day* seems to bear a greater resemblance to 1968.) What is at stake in this narrative, despite appearances, is not an allusion to finitude—a widespread theme during that period of the great ascendancy and fashion of the philosophy of existence; though Blanchot (as we know from other indications) was able to intuit, beyond the widely known Existentialist tenets, the thought then unknown in France and even in Germany of what may be called "the last Heidegger."[9] *The Madness of the Day* might therefore be said to be free from any temporal limitations in the current sense of the term, were it not for the fact that unfreedom (but an unfreedom less free than any determinism and any tragedy—a hellish unfreedom) is the intent of this text, as it runs through Blanchot's entire *œuvre* in a manner that is both renewal and repetition. In this renewal that is also a redundance, the presence of the present is (for lack of room, lack of land) immobilized. Day that does not pass. At the heart of the time that passes, nothing goes on, nothing comes up. All is always memory and threat. The flow of instants snags on transitions that spin around on themselves, recommence the Same. Iteration of a tale telling the tale itself. "I am neither knowing nor unknowing. I have known joyous moments, to say the least: I am alive, and this life gives me the greatest pleasure." This text occurs on page 9 and reappears on page 32: "I am not learned; I am not ignorant. I have known joys. That is saying too little. I told them the whole story."[10] The whole story turns on these joyous moments. A movement without outside, ex-pulsion without emptiness to receive the diaspora. "The void really disappointed me." A movement maintained in a maintenance that, in a human Self, is suffocation in self. The madness of the now, madness of the day. The madness of Auschwitz, which does not succeed in passing. Is the structure of the present—the actual, the Today—like this? The infernal. The infernal that shows itself in Auschwitz, but that lies hidden in the temporality of time, maintaining it.

The madness of day is not, then, related in order to complain about the non-sense that our reasonable conduct rubs shoulders with, nor to expose the discomfiture of humanist, virile humanity, surprised by the finitude of being. It is not the "madness of men" whom "night pierces," who, impatient to dominate and conquer, fail in their enterprises and "see their projects come to naught." It has nothing to do with these hackneyed phrases. Quite to the contrary, a different madness, like a distant drone of aircraft in the silence, lurks at the very heart of the joys, the day, and the unshakeable happiness described in the opening lines of our text.

What, then, is this happiness? The stability—the positivity—of the world posited before any thesis, rests behind all agitation and all desire, sustaining—or enveloping or including—all absurdity. A world confirming itself even in these ready-made phrases on the absurdity of the world. "The cool of the night, the stability of the earth made me breathe and rest upon the exhilaration" even "when I felt my life falling apart." A stability dominating time, which suspends its flight. Does it not roll itself up into hours—the meanders of presence—into good hours, lasting duration, permanence that reserves a place for death itself? A suppression of time *qua* event in time. This sudden turn borne by the syntax is not non-sense. "When I die (perhaps in a short while) I will experience great pleasure." *Perhaps in a short while*: the author's parenthetical remark suggests the inevitable return of the hour, the infallibility of the duly appointed hour. In Blanchot's mode of expression, the *prima facie* sense of a phrase or simple word resounds, descending or rising to the various levels to which it is given over by writing, despite the latter's power of fixation.

A repose of the world, or permanence of the Same, of which consciousness is perhaps but the pendant and emphasis: consciousness, in which every event—however overpowering—sets itself up as a state of the soul, and settles into place. "Whatever happens suits me," just as the forms of consciousness fit into the unity of one's "I think." All is in harmony: it is Europe! It is security. It is the inalienable. "I see this day, outside of which it

(the world) is nothing. Who could take that away from me?"
Only on the outside is there imperfection that shows itself to
me. I am *subject*, i.e. *absolutely lodged* and invulnerable. "I have a
roof, lots of people don't. I don't have leprosy." Death has its
hour—which it neither shatters nor overturns. The narrator was
to be shot in the madness of the world (which immediately
recovered its equilibrium, by the way); he was placed "with his
back to the wall," but the rifles that were supposed to shoot him
did not fire. Nothing stopped: as earlier, in the case of Thomas
the Obscure who drowned and did not drown, and as later in
L'attente L'oubli, in which affirmation and negation will be not
disjoined but conjoined. Death is lived as an event in life, in
which one experiences the lowering of the body into the ground,
its rotting-away, its reduction to the skeletal state or its dis-
section in a medical school. Death, which was to be the fading-
away of life, confirms the being of life in its generality of pure
being, and becomes part of it. Generality of pure being: the
biological and spiritual finality of the organic body no longer
deflects that ontology of presence from its abstract object. The
body knows itself to be pure water or pure burning. Nothingness
lived in being, and, as it were, the maturation of being. But then
that inevitable presence of the day becomes the aggressivity of
the day, and being in this day becomes weariness. This is the
last extremity of that stability of the earth, that harmony, that
happiness. The weariness of our old Europe, subversion at the
heart of its order. But what is denied is, in this same movement,
confirmed. Happiness besieges unhappiness, promising it a tearing loose, a way out, tiring it out. "In the worst moments of
unhappiness, I have been happy." "That discovery was not agree-
able." Weariness keeps recurring in the text: the void fills itself
with itself, repose doesn't settle down. Weariness—precisely.
There is no progressive dialectic, in which the moments of the
story spring up in their newness, before contradicting their
freshness by all they conserve. The circular return of the
Identical does not even follow a long-term cycle. It is a twirling
on the spot: happiness is obsessed in its very permanence, the

[margin note: note this allusion to Blanchot's experience.]

outbreak of madness sinks back into madness, into oppression, into an unbreathable interiority without exterior. Is madness a way out, or is the way out madness? Extreme consciousness would seem to be the consciousness of there being no way out; thus it would be not the outside, but the idea of the outside, and, so, obsession. An outside conceived of in the impossibility of the outside—thought producing the desire for the impossible outside. In which respect it is madness, or our religious condition.

Extreme consciousness is <u>obsession, suffocation, oppression, being crushed against a wall</u>. There is no wisdom; there is nothing to do. An infernal moment of that madness. "It is hell"—and not some metaphor for the horrible, but a burning without consumption. Like a diabolical mockery of the burning bush; the perception of an external threat that is not external. The hyenas howl, but those howls are only the cries of the one who hears them. A death to die of, and an impossible death. Death stripped of all mystery, in a world in which it corresponds to a confinement that is the meaning of matter itself. Being-toward-death for the earth and for water: the hole of nothingness—previously the only way out—is blocked by being tied [*noué*] in a knot [*nœud*] without dénouement, losing the meaning that tragedy still conferred upon it. In death, nothing is resolved [*se dénoue*]. The corpses that would litter the stage at the end of the Shakespearean tragedy no longer ease the ontological atmosphere. This narrative of the subterranean life that the after-death becomes is reworking, in modernity, of the story of Ulysses' visit to Hades, but in a manner that conveys its true horror.

3 On the Transparency that Wounds

But the day is not just the synchrony of succession, presence within which time sinks away, rolling itself into hours without anything being blurred, and in which blurring itself has its hour. Day is not just the emphasis of an existence that, by dint of being, shows itself and resounds and breaks forth in the form of consciousness. Consciousness, as clarity and vision, is also a modality of being that distances itself from itself, that, as representation, no longer weighs upon itself, while remaining true to its own standards in the transparency of truth: a transparency in which the screens and shadows that create contrasts and confine being within contradictions are dissolved, dissipated. A transparency in which being transforms itself into truth. The idea that this openness of truth, this clarity, attaining the transparency of the void, can wound the retina like glass breaking on the eye whose sight it sharpens—and that this wound is nonetheless sought after as lucidity and a sobering up: here again we have the madness of the day. The infinitely repeated iteration of madness desired as the light of day—and of day that wounds the eye that seeks it. "I almost lost my eyesight, someone having smashed glass on my eyes"—that is the central symbol of the Madness of the Day.

What is suggested is not the crisis of the sort of knowledge that, being prolonged and sought after by action, endangers the spirit that is liberated thereby. Knowledge is not denounced here merely in its technical essence by the death it spreads, and by the difficulties and the world-weariness to which it ultimately leads. It is truth with its happiness, self-evidence itself, that turn against their source—all the more fatally so, in that they are inevitably attractive and sought after. Is it perhaps in the transparency of knowledge, the appearing of a content, the very appearing of which already threatens the truth of its eventual later appearances? Or, harder yet, the skeleton of inassimilable forms that take shape in the process in which intellectualized, mathematized and dominated matter is affirmed—forms that assail the intellect, requiring of it an account it cannot furnish? Logical forms "without rule or goal," not governed by the principle, the undiscoverable principle? This is where we must situate the encounter with the law that the narrator does not succeed in forcing into dialogue, for the law, even if it is reasonable, is not saying [*dire*], but a necessity that imposes itself without speaking and that is deaf to all discourse—that is, to all apology, plea, or complaint. Perhaps this is the place in which to evoke the wound from which Leon Chestov,[11] stricken by the very necessity in which reasoned and reasoning reason [*la raison raisonnée et la raison raisonnante*] triumph, bleeds throughout all his works.

But the wound of transparency can be more wounding still. In the depths of the rational concept which is, according to Hegel, the transparency of thought itself, language, obscured by disturbances of its genealogy, explodes—constantly wounding the eye with the particles, or phantasms, that dance in the transparent void. This is the lucidity for which the mind determines the outer boundary. The more knowledge allows this boundary to expand, the tighter it becomes. There is no outside jurisdiction! Obviously one cannot "bring suit."[12] None is authorized. No more religion. The permanence of metaphysics (and the invitation to worship that, in Europe, resounds within it), those announcements to the effect that "*you want this too,*"[13] you, too, are oriented, in an irrecusable and unconscious way, without "objectifying intentionality," toward God—that permanence is but the obstinacy in conferring a meaning in the place where "clarity had lost all good sense," where clarity has consisted precisely in spiriting meaning away by sublimating it, and where the "going one better" of that disappearance of meaning consists in continuing its promotion to clarity.

> In the end, I grew convinced that I was face to face with the madness of the day. That was the truth: the light going mad, clarity had lost all good sense; it assailed me irrationally, without control, without purpose. That discovery bit straight through my life.[14]

A sought-after aggressivity. To the madness of the day which assails us in this manner there corresponds the desire for the day, a mad desire. The power of Reason, a master strong as death, according to Hegel; a master stronger than death, whom one does not escape through death, and with whom there is no reconciliation. A desire for water and air, but a desire desiring thirst itself, and the unbreathable. "I could neither look nor not look."[15] The impossible does not disappear as that which is self-contradictory. It is impossible in the sense in which we say this life is impossible: impossible although it is. Being realizes the impossible: an exile without space to receive the exiled.

The light that has come to us from Greece is not, on this view, true clarity. Self-consciousness, won by our history, is not a sobering up. It is always still drunk. Reason seeks an awakening as something beyond all vigilance. A lucidity more lucid than all lucidity, which, already a state, is already the state. Exaltation of vision under the threat that extinguishes it. Or, conversely, under the gauze where the afflicted eye has taken shelter, the wound is still contact with the light of seven days. The light of seven days of creation still not hidden by the compromises of history—a first light, intolerable and necessary. Transcendence in immanence, or strangulation of transcendence and recourse to the "fraudulent sleep"[16] of drugs? Is it certain that we are thus being told stories concerning only the anguish of intellectuals, or the difficulty of writing? Has Blanchot not related or foreseen a suffering *without any way out* in the absolute sense of the term? One always pushes someone back into the non-space, the over-crowded places already occupied. Above and beyond suffering, hell is this inverted space, this impasse of eternalized time, this distortion of Pure Reason, its intuitions and its categories. Madness of the day. An irrevocable voice says: "There is nothing to be done." There is nothing to be done: this is announced not in *one* abstract proposition, but by the condition, or uncondition, of humanity.

4 A Baby Carriage

Relation to the other—a last way out. From one end to the other of the story, this relation is present. The loss of loved ones was the very shock that interrupted happiness, or, more precisely, transformed its felicity into the suffocating embrace of solitude, the one reliable clasp. The little scene in which, in front of the courtyard door, a man steps back to let a baby carriage through, is the event of an advent—that is, the moment when something abnormal ensues: one person withdraws before the other, one *is* for the other. Whence the narrator's lightheartedness, which seems to lift him above being. A misleading event, which is immediately confused with the dark chill of anonymity— with the cosmic coldness chilling the narrator, who looks into the depths of a dark courtyard, to the bone. The silence of those infinite spaces ... [17] Compared with the immensity of being, and the masses who have mutually slaughtered one another, what is the uncertain movement of someone who lets you pass ahead of him? Such a thought is but a commonplace! Unworthy of a distinguished mind; but it sings incessantly in the silence that scorns and stifles it. It is in vain that we dismantle the *I* that is concerned about itself—perseverance in being, the *conatus*— in order to reveal a "devotion" to the other person in its depths, to the point of canceling out egotism in its modality of mutual kindness in the graces of the Western world's polite society: suffering *for* the other and *in* the other does not reach disinterestment. The altruistic consciousness returns to itself. Suffering for and in others—is others making me suffer! "That huge other gave me back to myself far more than I should have liked."[18] And that ends in the temptation of murder. True, the others, "their least discomfort becomes an infinite evil to me," and "yet, if I must, I sacrifice them deliberately, I deprive them of all happy feelings (I occasionally kill them)."

Whence the relation with the other as a consolidation of oneself (to the point of becoming "tough"). Self-denial is but a return to European individualism and a hardening of the self. *I* is stronger than the others! "I'll have to bury a few of them before I go," "my existence has a surprising solidity." It is in terms of *self-consciousness* that, in the final analysis, our grand philosophical tradition expresses and envelops the relation to the other: the other as willed, however, in his or her "otherwise," willed as a God, willed with a will that is religion itself. A willing that becomes dulled: "at the same time," within me something soon ceased willing. *In terms of consciousness*, but of a consciousness without interiority. The condition of an insect beneath the gaze of the "somber spirit of reading"; a simple relay in a system reduced to the act of sending messages between poles, at which points in turn the only activity is that of the switchboard operator. A formalism—or profession—or ontological status to which the narrator is reduced in the clinic that took him in when transparency wounded him. There is this same formalism in his relation to the work of culture, in which the human becomes universalized, in which the multidimensional anonymity of Scripture tempts us with its unknown appearance. "I have read many books." Indeed so. But "when I disappear, little by little, all these volumes will change." There can be no book—without my exegesis. But apparently exegesis is a mere distraction that Europeans are getting tired of. Does Blanchot think there is no longer any book? No reading, no writing, no expression. There is nothing to penetrate, no interiority, no depth. Everything in being is irremediably solid. Forms endlessly envelop envelopes. No God! Within the split nucleus there are but more nuclei. Burrows leading down to more burrows. False depths of the subterranean in which exegesis, going from book to book, ventures forth like a librarian crossing over narrow walkways; but, in his crossing, executing only the passage from one term to another, one sign to another, without a signified. The intelligence in which people communicate is a game in which counters of the known are exchanged. Already it is the boredom of space travel: the astronaut, astonished at the sight of things never seen before, has never heard the speech of a non-Adamite humanity—the only speech that could be truly new.

In the clinic, where the focus of interest is on "blood," you are scrutinized from outside, and cannot escape into the secretive. You cannot draw the outside—which exposes you to your fellows—in: the verso is no match for the recto. Exposure to one another in relations whose terms deny one another. My living space is a place that I take away from others, and even my wretchedness is a provocation, an accusation and a solicitation, as if it wore "justice on [its] clothing." Justice totally turned toward the outside, but an outside without any way out.

Nothing escapes the reciprocity of the system. Escape is possible only through the fraudulent illusions of drugs. But you are always caught, always brutally torn from fraudulent sleep, from that which is not position, not thesis: from that which carries you off, as does libido. Why is that sleep fraudulent?[19] What distinguishes being from illusion? The being of beings [*l'être de l'étant*] does not make light of its privileges.

And what of the political order? And what of the door opened up by charity? The marvelous transcendence of man *qua* citizen, the great hope of the Enlightenment? Indeed, "I was unknown in the other, but I was sovereign," a subject yet a prince, a free man among free men. That sovereignty shared equally is nonetheless a power—the free man's power to lapidate, criminal hostility toward the singular. Alternating violence perpetrated by some and persecution undergone by others. The conceptual, legal justification of power, the anonymous discourse of the Law, can offer no consolation. The law does not enter into the private conversation of dialogue. "To tempt the law, I called softly to her, 'Come here; let me see you face to face.' (For a moment I wanted to take her aside.) It was a foolhardy appeal. What would I have done if she had answered?"

It is true that the Law can speak another language—the language of man's servant: that is the law of personalist humanism, of fraternity or even charity. But her diacony, going as far as servitude, is an incessant reproach, even if she is capable at times of compensating a man thus overwhelmed by the enjoyable trifles of taking liberties with the servant-girl, as if the human being were "the kind of man who is satisfied with a knee," and did not risk beguiling his desires by contenting himself with cheap eroticism or the comforts of a Sunday at the movies. For all in all that law of human elevation does no more than fix the eye upon a part of the wall between the window and the ceiling, staring with fierce intensity, to hail the Day or Heaven in fear and trembling. This is the demystification of height, after that of the depths. There is, in this text from 1948, a troubling premonition of everything that would be fully revealed and parade around the public square, in all its inanity and madness, twenty years later. The other [*autrui*], the only point of access to an outside, is closed. The other stabs a knife into my flesh and derives a sense of spirituality from declaring himself guilty. The idea of bearing the other, suffering in him (Celan's sublime expression, "The world is no more, I shall have to carry you") turns into a comedy in an insane asylum, in which the patients have fun taking rides on the back of the narrator, on all fours. The transcendence of the intersubjective is oppression in the highest degree, and altruism stultifying. The *I* suffocates in its dray-horse being.

5 Of Two Who Are Three

Of what does this text speak, if not of the no exit, the closure of doors and windows and air vents, the sealing off of death by being, and, within that inside devoid of an outside, the incessant oppression of expulsion: "going back into the wall, or straying into a thicket of flint." This oppression is not just the suffering of a human soul in an inhuman society, or that of a finite mind jolted by being, which is unaware of its existence. Here, man's humanity is but the stage for a plot without dénouement: being inextricable, it does not succeed in working itself out into a story, but rather works itself up in its attempt to do so. The meaning of the story is lost: what happens does not succeed in happening, does not go into a story.

"The meaning of the story is lost." Once again, a banal phrase resonates in Blanchot's text with a sort of piling up of its meaning—from the lowest to the highest, to the level at which (beyond the famous absurdity of existence and contingency of events) the end of the literature of the ineffable bursts forth: the end of the literature of the "fable," the end of language, i.e. the end of that verbal synchrony by which all disorder was still able to pass for a different order;[20] the end of those tales in which incompatibilities, in their difference, could still share a common written page, even if, as words, and as falling from the lips, they could still be lost.

But the telling of the story is also impossible because the language is neither expression nor interrogation, but a cross-examination. One's relationship with the other is one of recourse: you turn yourself over to the doctors, who keep watch over you. The ophthalmologist and the psychologist check vision and thought; they check and they spy upon you. In their helping objectivity they are the accomplices to order, i.e. the established order. They prompt you to tell the story, to adopt the mode of existence that can be resumed in the fable—excluding the extra-vagant. Logical order is re-established by an order. The invitation to narrate is a summons. "Of course neither of them was the chief of police. But because there were two of them, there were three." It suffices that there be two for the powers to be served. To tell a story, to speak, is already to make a police report. "No stories, never again"—these are the last words of the text. But still madness. The very presence of this text belies the ultimate freedom of refusal. A text, a texture, a weave, a work! Despite all refusal, somewhere in the brain, "it keeps on knitting."

Notes

PROPER NAMES

Foreword

1. [I.e., Heidegger's Nazi affiliations and his apparent insensitivity to the fate of the victims of the Holocaust.—Trans.]
2. [Probably directed against Bergson. See his *Evolution Créatrice,* Ch. III, in *Œuvres* (Paris: Presses Universitaires de France, 1970), 694, 1338. Bergson maintains that all "disorder" is but a different order. See also Levinas, *Collected Philosophical Papers,* trans. A. Lingis (Dordrecht: Martinus Nijhoff, 1987), 166 n. 18, and *On Maurice Blanchot,* "Exercises on 'The Madness of the Day,'" note 20 below.—Trans.]
3. *Metaphysical Journal,* trans. B. Wall (London: Rockliff, 1952), 210–211. [Translation slightly altered.—Trans.]

1 Poetry and Resurrection: Notes on Agnon

1. [Hebrew: love of Israel.—Trans.]
2. [A covert allusion to the rabbinic saying of Ben Bag-bag in reference to the Torah (*Pirke Avot* 5, 22): Turn it and turn it for everything is in it.—Trans.]
3. [Hebrew: figurative language.—Trans.]
4. The solidity of the substratum, of the statue (of the monument and the monumental), in which that ontology, that comprehension of being, seeks a refuge from nothingness. In the story of the dog Balak (Chap. X, 2), Agnon narrates that quest in the guise of the parable of the wild animals who prefer the destiny of stuffed animals, assured of

an eternity in the museums, to the hazards of a life threatened with pure and simple nothingness, by starvation or the cruelty of stronger beasts. Perhaps this fate of the stuffed animal is that of the "historical figure."

5. [Levinas gives no indication of what work of Agnon's he is quoting.—Trans.]

6. [This work has apparently not yet been translated into English.—Trans.]

7. [Genesis 22:7.—Trans.]

8. [This appears to be Levinas's own translation. See (in Hebrew) *The Complete Stories of Shmuel Josef Agnon*, vol. 8, *The Fire and the Wood: The Sign* (Tel Aviv: Schocken, 1962), 303. The second part of the quotation (after the ellipsis) is from the following page.—Trans.]

9. My emphasis.

10. This quotation is followed, in the text, by the following passage.

In the *Conversations of Maharan*, blessed be his memory, it is related that one day this just man heard a preacher from Lemberg who snapped his fingers at the moment of death, as if he were performing a clever feat in leaving this world of sadness. [See Agnon, *The Complete Stories*, vol. 8, 304.—Trans.]

11. [ibid., 302.—Trans.]

2 Martin Buber and the Theory of Knowledge

1. [Quotations from Martin Buber's works are cited in the text using the following abbreviations:

BM: *Between Man and Man*, trans. R. G. Smith (New York: The Macmillan Company, 1965)

IT: *I and Thou*, trans. R. G. Smith (New York: Charles Scribner's Sons, 1958)

KM: *The Knowledge of Man*, ed. M. Friedman, trans. M. Friedman and R. G. Smith (New York: Harper & Row, Torchbook edition, 1966)

Levinas's quotations sometimes differ somewhat from sources.— Trans.]

2. [Doubtless an allusion to Psalm 36:10 (36:9 in Christian Bibles).—Trans.]

3. Mr. Maurice S. Friedman's article, "Martin Buber's *Theory of Knowledge*," which appeared in *The Review of Metaphysics*, sets forth the essential traits of Buber's epistemology with clarity and penetration, but does not show their affinity to contemporary philosophical trends. These trends, while they do not make the I–Thou into a central theme, have broken with the subject–object relation and the ontology that sustained it. Specifically, Buber was certainly not the theoretician of the "It." See also, in that article, the excellent bibliography of works that, running parallel to Buber or under his influence, were dedicated to the "I–Thou."

4. See the opuscule *Urdistanz und Relation* [available in English as "Distance and Relation," in *The Knowledge of Man*; see above, note 1.—Trans.].

5. [The French expression "cela me dit quelque chose" is a familiar phrase, often rendered as "that rings a bell" or "that reminds me of something." Literally, it means "that tells me something."—Trans.]

6. [Here the French version in *Noms propres* is clearly in error. It reads: "Pour Husserl, la représentation de la chose en personne tranche sur la représentation et m'engage. …" But it is Buber, not Husserl, that holds this view. The earlier German version ("Martin Buber und die Erkenntnistheorie," in *Martin Buber. Philosophen des 20. Jahrhunderts* [ed. P. A. Schlipp and M. Friedman, Stuttgart: Kohlhammer, 1963], 119–134) contains the following sentence, missing from the French, which I have restored in my translation: "Für Husserl ist die leibliche Darstellung des Dings nur eine Art der Vorstellung." The next German sentence begins: "Für Buber die Darstellung …"—Trans.]

7. [In *The Knowledge of Man*, 149–167.—Trans.]

8. As Bergson assuredly thought, when he began his 1888 essay with the words: "We express ourselves of necessity in words …" [See *Time and Free Will: An Essay on the Immediate Data of Consciousness*, trans. F. L. Pogson (New York: 1910).—Trans.]

3 Dialogue with Martin Buber

1. [See *The Philosophy of Martin Buber* (La Salle: Open Court, 1967), 723. I have translated Levinas's French translation of Buber's

reply, which differs slightly from M. Friedman's translation of Buber's original German.—Trans.]

2. [Buber's eighty-fifth birthday.—Trans.]

3. [The tradition of Maine de Biran, French philosopher (1766–1824).—Trans.]

4. "Great is the mouthful" (of nourishment).

5. The doctors of the Talmud.

6. A term from Deuteronomy 6:5, which is, in this form, hapax. Its direct meaning translates into "your excess" or "your strength."

7. "In einem freudigen und freundlichen Gedächtnis." An interplay of sound and sense impossible in French. [In English as well.—Trans.]

8. In French in the text.

4 Paul Celan: From Being to the Other

[Since Levinas's interpretation of Celan is often closely tied to the wording of the French translation he quotes, I have chosen to follow it in the main, but have consulted the German original as well, and occasionally moved the text in its direction. In the following notes I shall give the corresponding page number of Rosemarie Waldrop's English translation (*Paul Celan/Collected Prose* [New York: The Sheep Meadow Press, 1986]), abbreviated as RW, though I rarely have been able to quote it verbatim, and then the page number of Celan's original German (*Paul Celan, Gessammelte Werke*, vol. 3 [Frankfurt am M.ain: Suhrkamp, 1983], abbreviated as PC.—Trans.]

1. Each of these visits "changed him [Heidegger] deeply" according to an unquestionable testimony I received in these very words.

2. RW 18; PC 169ff.

3. [See also 131, below, for another comment on impersonal (or "neuter") language.—Trans.]

4. RW 44; PC 197. [The French text reads as follows: "Le poème va d'une traite au-devant de cet autre qu'il suppose à même d'être rejoint, dégagé—délivré—vacant peut-être …". Levinas quotes the French translation by André du Bouchet "Entretien dans la Montagne," in *Strette* (Paris: Mercure de France, 1971), 191. This translation differs greatly from that of Rosemarie Waldrop, and is essential to Levinas's interpretation. The German original of Celan's 1960 speech, which seems to me to justify the du Bouchet translation, is as follows. The poem "hält unentwegt auf jenes 'Andere' zu, das es sich als erreichbar,

als freizusetzen, als vakant vielleicht, und dabei ihm, dem Gedicht ...
zugewandt denkt."—Trans.]
5. "A matter of hands," Celan writes to Hans Bender.
6. RW 50; PC 198.
7. RW 53; PC 201.
8. RW 48; PC 196.
9. RW 48; PC 197.
10. RW 51; PC 199.
11. RW 45; PC 194. [The last sentence quoted is in French in
Celan. It means: "Poetry, too, rushes ahead of us."—Trans.]
12. Transcendence through poetry—is this serious? It is after all a
distinctive trait of the modern spirit, or of modern rationalism.
Alongside the mathematization of facts, by tracing them upward to
the level of form, there is the *schematization* (in the Kantian sense) of
intelligibles by the descent into sensibility. Formal, pure concepts,
when put to the test in the concrete, the impure, resonate (or reason)
differently, and take on new meanings. The exposure of the categories
of the understanding to time certainly limited the rights of reason, but
it also uncovered a physics at the basis of mathematical logic. The
abstract idea of substance became the principle of the constancy of
mass, and the empty concept of community became the principle of
reciprocal interaction.—In Hegel, do not the figures of the dialectic
delineate themselves vigorously by *playing an active role* in the history
of humanity?—Is not Husserl's phenomenology a way of schematizing
the real within the unsuspected horizons of sensible subjectivity? Just as
formal logic is to be referred back to the concretization of subjectivity,
so the world of perception and history, in its objectivity, is accused of
abstraction, if not of formalism—and becomes the vital lead to the discovery of horizons of meaning, within which it will begin to signify
with true signification. In reading the recent and very curious and
beautiful work on psychosis [*La Psychose*] (Louvain/Paris: Nauwelaerts,
1971) by Alphonse de Waelhens, for whom Husserl and Heidegger
held no secrets, I got the impression that Freudianism does nothing
but return the phenomenological sensible (which is still logical or pure
in its images, its oppositions, its covergences and its iterations) to a
kind of ultimate sensibility, in which the difference between the sexes,
in particular, determines the possibilities of a *schematization* without
which the *sensible significations* would remain as abstract as the idea of
cause outside temporal succession was before the *Critique of Pure*

Reason. A whole drama lurks within the mathematician's combinations and the metaphysician's play of pure concepts. The critique of *pure* reason continues!

    13. RW 52; PC 200.

    14. RW 46; PC 195.

    15. RW 49; PC 198.

    16. Simone Weil is able to write: "Father, tear this body and this soul away from me, to make of them your things, and let nothing remain of me eternally but that tearing-away itself."

    17. RW 50; PC 199.

    18. RW 42–43; PC 192.

    19. RW 51; PC 199.

    20. "Doch Kunst ist Eröffnung des Seins des Seienden." Heidegger, *Einführung in die Metaphysik* (Tübingen: Max Niemeyer Verlag, 1953), 101.

    21. [See Leviticus 18:28.—Trans.]

    22. RW 19; PC 169–170.

    23. RW 54; PC 202.

    24. RW 51; PC 199.

    25. RW 55; PC 202.

    26. RW 51; PC 199.

5 Jeanne Delhomme: Penelope, or Modal Thought

    1. [Here I follow the text of the original printing of this review, in *Critique* (Dec., 1967, vol. 247), p. 1032, which has "manifestation" rather than "manifestement" ("clearly") as in the later (1976) text.—Trans.]

    2. [The French phrase, "fait 'des histoires' et l'Histoire" (makes trouble, and History), loses its pun in translation.—Trans.]

    3. The term "intentionality," which seems to me quite helpful in understanding Madame Delhomme's intent, is infrequent in her text. Curiously, despite the concision, subtlety and rigor with which she conducts her analysis (commanding an overview of the texts because she knows them in great detail, having taught them to an entire generation), it never becomes "intentional analysis." The descriptive techniques of Husserlian and Heideggerian phenomenology are ignored. The phenomenology that speaks in her work is dialectic—Hegelian and Platonic. The *Parmenides* and the *Sophist* are present on

every page. Her exposition unfolds in a series of long propositions, organized internally with semicolons and colons. Each proposition constitutes the complete development of an idea. The severity of the form, which does not, however, cut away content, renders the blunt frankness of a rare direct avowal all the more striking.

4. [The 1976 version of this text, published in *Noms propres*, has "irruption." I follow the original 1967 version published in *Critique*, which has "interruption."—Trans.]

5. Jeanne Delhomme, *La pensée et le réel. Critique de l'ontologie* (Paris: Presses Universitaires de France, Collection "Epiméthée," 1967), 54–55.

6. Ibid., 148.

7. [See Jeanne Delhomme's *Temps et destin. Essai sur André Malraux* (Paris: Gallimard, 1955).—Trans.]

8. [A well-known verse from "Le Voyage," the last poem in Charles Baudelaire's *Fleurs du mal.*—Trans.]

9. *Le jeu comme symbole du monde* (Paris: Les Editions de Minuit, 1966).

6 Jacques Derrida: Wholly Otherwise

1. [As it is called in Husserl's *Ideas*, paragraph 83.—Trans.]

2. [In English in the original.—Trans.]

3. [The expression, frequently used by Levinas, is from Paul Valéry's poem "Cantique des Colonnes." See Paul Valéry, *Œuvres*, vol. 1 (Paris: Gallimard, 1957), 118.—Trans.]

4. [See above, 51.—Trans.]

5. [*Eigenheit* refers to those qualities that are peculiar to an individual; *Eigentum*, to individual property, ownership.—Trans.]

6. [*Speech and Phenomena* (Evanston: Northwestern University Press, 1973), 95; in French, "Est-ce sûr?" See *La voix et le phénomène* (Paris: Presses Universitaires de France, 1967), 106.—Trans.]

7. [See *On Maurice Blanchot*, "The Servant and Her Master," 146 below.—Trans.]

8. [See *The Sophist*, 241d. Levinas alludes to the same "parricide" in *Humanisme de l'autre homme* (Montpellier: Fata Morgana, Livre de Poche, [1972] 1987), 10.—Trans.]

9. [For further clarification of the relationship between meaning and intuition (or presence), see Levinas's *Meaning and Sense*, which was

published in 1972, only one year before "Wholly Otherwise," and is available in English as Chapter 6 of Levinas's *Collected Philosophical Papers*, trans. A. Lingis (Dordrecht: Martinus Nijhoff, 1987), 75–107, esp. 75–79.—Trans.]

10. An ambition that Kant very mischievously attributed to Salomon Maimon with respect to the critical philosophy, in his letter of March 28, 1789, to Reinhold. It is true that the two situations are in no way similar. For several reasons! [Simon Critchley, to whose 1991 translation of this piece the present translator is indebted, has discovered that the actual date of the letter is March 28, 1794, and explains the implications of Levinas's footnote in an extended footnote. See *Re-reading Levinas*, ed. R. Bernasconi and S. Critchley (Bloomington: Indiana University Press, 1991), 9–10, n. 11.—Trans.]

7 Edmond Jabès Today

1. [The untranslatable passage is: "le mot Dieu, entendu comme le mot 'oeil' ou écrit comme 'd'yeux'." *Dieu* (God) is a homonym of "d'yeux" (of eyes).—Trans.]

8 Kierkegaard: Existence and Ethics

1. [The notion of "poètes maudits" (accursed poets) evokes certain nineteenth-century figures, such as Rimbaud and Verlaine, whose scandalous writings and lifestyle made them notorious.—Trans.]

2. [See Martin Heidegger's *Being and Time* (New York: Harper & Row, 1962), 67.—Trans.]

3. Jean Wahl, the most complete, penetrating and philosophical of Kierkegaard's historians, recognizes this; for example, for the fundamental concept of anxiety. See *Études kierkegaardiennes* (Paris: 1938), 211, n. 2.

4. [Diacony, or deaconry, is derived from a Greek word meaning servant.—Trans.]

5. I wish to pay homage, on this occasion, to the magnificent *œuvre* of Max Picard, who spoke so profoundly of the metaphysical opening in the "human face," and to refer the reader to those texts. [See Chapter 10.—Trans.]

6. [Genesis 22:1–19.—Trans.]

7. [Genesis 18:1–33.—Trans.]

9 A Propos of "Kierkegaard vivant"

1. [In the series "Idées." It contains papers presented by J.-P. Sartre, G. Marcel, L. Goldman, M. Heidegger *in absentia*, K. Jaspers, J. Wahl, *et al.* The conference, organized by UNESCO in Paris, took place on April 21–23, 1964.—Trans.]

2. [I.e. "Kierkegaard: Existence and Ethics." See Chapter 8.—Trans.]

3. [Jeanne Hersch, one of the participants in the conference "Kierkegaard Vivant." Her presentation was titled "The Instant" (*Kierkegaard vivant*, 94–110).—Trans.]

4. [Genesis 22:1–19.—Trans.]

5. [Genesis 18:1–33.—Trans.]

6. [Beaufret (1907–1982), a Heideggerian philosopher who participated in the conference "Kierkegaard Vivant." Beaufret's participation took the form of a presentation and reading of a text he co-translated by Heidegger titled "The End of Philosophy and the Task of Thought," and some remarks during the discussion period.—Trans.]

10 Jean Lacroix: Philosophy and Religion

1. [Descartes, *Discours de la Méthode*, Seconde Partie (Paris: La Renaissance du Livre, 1928), 29. My translation.—Trans.]

2. [The French is "arrière-mondes," the standard French translation of Nietzsche's "Hinterweltern." See *Also sprach Zarathustra*, Part I, "Von den Hinterweltern." The usual English translation, "backworlds," is not very helpful.—Trans.]

3. See Nietzsche, *Morgenröthe*: "The historical refutation as definitive. Formerly one attempted to prove the non-existence of God; today one shows how the belief in God was able to arise and how that belief took on weight and importance. Hence the counterproof of the non-existence of God becomes superfluous." [*Nietzsches Werke*, vol. 5 (Leipzig: C. G. Naumann Verlag, 1906), 89.—Trans.]

4. [Léon Brunschvicg (1869–1944), whose philosophy of critical idealism dominated academic French philosophy during the student years of Sartre, Merleau-Ponty and Levinas, is the author of a study on Spinoza: *Spinoza et ses contemporains* (1923).—Trans.]

5. The Spinozan way of "explaining" images instead of seeking within them a knowledge (however embryonic) of the true, is in

Descartes, in whose writings the sensible is not the source of the true, but the sign of the useful.

6. The Spinozan enterprise cannot be reduced to this thesis, which is nonetheless a very important one; and Jean Lacroix, in agreement on this score with Sylvain Zac's thesis, finds in the *Treatise* the indication of a "non-philosophical" path to "salvation." See Sylvain Zac, *Spinoza et l'interprétation de l'Écriture* (Paris: Presses Universitaires de France, 1965).

7. [This piece was originally published in the journal *Critique* (see bibliographical note on p. xii) as a collective review of three works by Jean Lacroix. They are, in the order in which Levinas mentions them here: *Spinoza et le problème du salut* (Paris: Presses Universitaires de France, 1970); *Le sens de l'athéisme moderne* (Paris: Casterman, 6th edn., 1970); *La crise intellectuelle du catholicisme français* (Paris: Fayard, 1970).—Trans.]

8. [See Plato, *Republic*, 517 bc and 518 cd.—Trans.]

9. [The French is: *ce néant qui "néantit."* Doubtless Levinas is referring to Jean-Paul Sartre, who coined this verb, which occurs in the first chapter of *Being and Nothingness.*—Trans.]

10. *Apophansis* is Husserl's term for the formal logic of statements. *Epos*, Greek for word, utterance, prophecy, or poetry.

11. The Song of Songs, 5:15, translated, according to a new virtuality, as *Le Chant des chants*, by Henri Meschonnic, in *Les Cinq Rouleaux* [The Five Scrolls] (Paris: Gallimard, 1970).

12. This term translates the φρικη of Plato's *Phaedrus*, 251a. [French "frémissements."—Trans.]

13. [This latter expression occurs in Spinoza's *Ethics*, First Part, definition 3.—Trans.]

14. [Count Joseph de Maistre (1753–1821) and Viscount Louis de Bonald (1754–1840) were staunch defenders of ecclesiastic authority and monarchic principles.—Trans.]

11 Roger Laporte and the Still Small Voice

1. [This piece originally appeared as a review of Roger Laporte's *Une voix de fin silence* (A Still Small Voice) (Paris: Gallimard, 1966).—Trans.]

2. Jean Beaufret. See Chapter 9, note 6.

3. [French philosopher and Christian mystic (1909–1943), whose views on Judaism and the "Old Testament" are critically examined by Levinas in "Simone Weil contre la Bible," *Difficile Liberté*, 3rd edn. (Paris: Albin Michel, [1963] 1976), 189–200.—Trans.]

12 Max Picard and the Face

1. [Gaston Bachelard (1888–1962), French philosopher, author of works that cut across the traditional disciplines: e.g. *Psychanalyse du feu, L'eau et les rêves.*—Trans.]
2. [See Baudelaire's "Correspondances," the fourth poem in his *Fleurs du mal.*—Trans.]
3. [This sentence ends with a colon in French, but the absence of quotation marks or indentation would seem to indicate that Levinas is giving his own version of the story, which blends in with the latter's philosophical interpretation, particularly toward the end. Levinas's version of this story is quoted by Catherine Chalier, who sets it in the context of Maimonides and the Talmud: see her *Pensées de l'éternité* (Paris: Éditions du Cerf, 1993).—Trans.]

13 The Other in Proust

1. [T. A. Ribot (1839–1916), psychologist tending toward physicalist explanations of mental phenomena.—Trans.]
2. [Here Levinas has incorporated the French title of *Remembrance of Things Past (À la recherche du temps perdu* is more literally "In Search of Lost Time") into the end of his sentence.—Trans.]
3. Édouard Estaunié (1862–1942), French novelist from Dijon.

14 Father Herman Leo Van Breda

1. [This piece, commemorating Van Breda's death, was published in the same issue of the society's *Bulletin*. See bibliographical note on p. xii.—Trans.]
2. E. Husserl, *Phänomenologische Psychologie*, vol. 9 of the *Gesammelte Werke* (The Hague: Martinus Nijhoff, 1962), 148.

15 Jean Wahl and Feeling

1. Jean Wahl, *Traité de métaphysique* (Paris: Payot, 1953; Plon, 1955).
2. Probably an oblique reference to André Gide's well-known novel, *Les nourritures terrestres*, which marks a hedonistic turn.
3. *Traité de métaphysique*, 73.
4. Ibid., 72.
5. Ibid., 277.
6. Ibid., 69, 259, 267 and elsewhere.
7. Ibid., 635.
8. Ibid., 357.
9. Ibid., 367.
10. Ibid., 700.
11. Ibid., 389.
12. Ibid., 180.
13. Ibid., 721.
14. Ibid., 702.
15. Ibid., 6.
16. [Diogenes the Cynic, who is said to have been seen wandering the Athenian streets at noon with a lit lamp, muttering: "I am looking for a man."—Trans.]
17. *Traité de métaphysique*, 268.

16 Nameless

1. [Rural French resistance groups during the Second World War.—Trans.]

ON MAURICE BLANCHOT

1 The Poet's Vision

1. *L'Espace littéraire* (Paris: Gallimard, 1955). [*The Space of Literature,* trans. Ann Smock (Lincoln: University of Nebraska Press, 1982).]

2. [Maurice Blanchot, more than twenty years later, comments on this sentence: "but [he] ended his sentence with an exclamation point, which modified its meaning, possibly reversing it" (*Notre compagne clandestine,* in: F. Laruelle (ed.) *Texts pour Emmanuel Levinas* [Paris: Jean-Michel Place, 1980], my translation). And in addition to the ironic nuance noted by Blanchot, Levinas's next two sentences would seem to restrict "everyone" to Marxists and Heideggerians.—Trans.]

3. See esp. the end of Heidegger's *Letter on Humanism.*

4. ["Néanit" is a coinage of Jean-Paul Sartre's. See *Being and Nothingness,* Part One, Ch. 1, passim.—Trans.]

5. ["*Sans figure*" could be interpreted as either "without face" or "without figure"; if the former, Blanchot is using a familiar French word for face, less dignified than "*visage,*" which is the term used by Max Picard and Levinas.—Trans.]

6. [This rather puzzling passage seems to indicate that Levinas ascribes Blanchot's esthetic affinities with Heidegger to an intuitive commonality or "presentiment." See below, 159.—Trans.]

7. *L'Espace littéraire,* 235–236. [I quote from Ann Smock's exemplary translation, *The Space of Literature,* 226, slightly altered.—Trans.]

8. [*The Space of Literature*, 247 n., slightly altered. Levinas, in his quotation from Blanchot, has omitted the words in brackets.—Trans.]

9. [See *Proper Names*, Chapter 6, n. 3, above.—Trans.]

10. [The reference is to *Vorträge und Aufsätze* (Lectures and Essays) (Pfullingen: Neske, 1954), which includes the 1951 lecture "Bauen Wohnen Denken" ("Building Dwelling Thinking") and the 1950 lecture, "Das Ding" ("The Thing"). These two pieces are available in English in *Poetry, Language, Thought* (New York: Harper & Row, [1971] 1975).—Trans.]

11. [Here Levinas is paraphrasing Heidegger's distinction between abstract space and the thing-place manifold (e.g. the bridge) Heidegger takes to be its source. See *Poetry, Language, Thought*, 154ff.—Trans.]

2 The Servant and Her Master

1. Perhaps. We are not dealing with allegorical figures. The sensible fullness of these figures, however bare and, as it were, abstract, is intact. We find ourselves involved with thicknesses and masses spread out in dimensions, and according to an order that is their own, raising problems, as in a delirium, scarcely communicable once the fever has passed and day dawned. That is the unique configuration of Blanchot's literary space. The meaning of his world concerns our own. But interpretation is what such a work rejects; a work that is perhaps entirely the breaking through of that envelope with which non-contradictory *saying* attempts to surround all movement. Should we try to immobilize a few of its shimmering lights, without fearing that we may extinguish them in the process? Here, all must be said in the "perhaps" mode, in the manner of Blanchot himself, when he tries to explain what has said itself in his books.

2. The page numbers in parentheses in the text refer to *L'attente L'oubli* [Waiting Forgetting] (Paris: Gallimard, 1962).

3. [See Heidegger, *Sein und Zeit*, 16th edn. (Tübingen: Max Niemeyer, 1986), 42.—Trans.]

4. No moral element intervenes in Blanchot to constitute this modality. It is neither to its poverty nor to persecution or disdain that it owes the privilege of disappearing from the horizon—of transcending it—and of responding from the depths of its absence only to the best. And yet there are moments when transcendence in Blanchot is made up of the uncertainty of presence itself, as if it had only been present "to keep from speaking. And then there would come the

moments when, the thread of their relationship having broken, she would recover her calm reality. At those times he could see more clearly in what an extraordinary state of weakness she was, from which she derived that authority that sometimes caused her to speak" (26). I have already said, above, that the word poetry, to me, means the rupture of the immanence to which language is condemned, imprisoning itself. I do not think that this rupture is a purely esthetic event. But the word poetry does not, after all, designate a species, the genus of which would be art. Inseparable from the verb, it overflows with prophetic meaning. [By "the verb" Levinas probably means the Greek verb *poiein*, to make, create, from which the term "poetry" is derived.—Trans.]

    5. [I.e. not in code.—Trans.]

    6. See Martin, *Logique contemporaine et formalisme* (Paris: Presses Universitaires de France, n.d.), 22ff.

3 A Conversation with André Dalmas

    1. Françoise Collin, *Maurice Blanchot et la question de l'écriture* (Paris: Gallimard, 1971).

    2. ["Ah! ne jamais sortir des Nombres et des Êtres!" (Ah! Never to leave Numbers and Beings). The last line of the poem "Le Gouffre," added to the 1868 edition as CII: see *Œuvres complètes* (Paris: Gallimard, 1961), 172.—Trans.]

    3. [*Thomas the Obscure*, trans. R. Lamberton (Barrytown: Station Hill Press, 1988). A translation of *Thomas l'obscur*, new version (Paris: Gallimard, 1950).—Trans.]

    4. [*L'attente, L'oubli* (Paris: Gallimard, 1962).—Trans.]

    5. [See Exodus 3:2.—Trans.]

    6. [Writer, literary critic, member of the Académie française, director of *La Nouvelle Revue Française*. His comments on language are to be found in *Les Fleurs de Tarbes* (Paris: Gallimard, 1941) and *Clef de la poésie* (Paris: Gallimard, 1944).—Trans.]

    7. See *Proper Names*, Chapter 10, note 2 above.—Trans.]

4 Exercises on "The Madness of the Day"

    1. [*La folie du jour* (Montpellier: Fata Morgana, 1973); *The Madness of the Day/La Folie du Jour*, trans. L. Davis (New York: Station Hill, 1981).—Trans.]

2. [Metaphor, from Greek *metaphora*: to carry across.—Trans.]

3. [In the (Greek) etymological sense of "from outside."—Trans.]

4. See my *Autrement qu'être, ou au-delà de l'essence* (The Hague: Martinus Nijhoff, 1974), 53, and *De l'existence à l'existent* (Paris: Vrin, [1974] 1986), 83ff. See also "La Réalité et son ombre," *Les Temps Modernes,* no. 38 (1948): 771–789. [*Otherwise than Being or Beyond Essence* (The Hague, Boston, London: Martinus Nijhoff, 1981), 41, and *Existence and Existents* (Dordrecht, Boston, London: Kluwer Academic, [1978] 1988), 52ff. See also "Reality and its Shadow," Chapter 1 of *Emmanuel Levinas: Collected Philosophical Papers* (Dordrecht, Boston, Lancaster: Martinus Nijhoff, 1987), 1–13.—Trans.]

5. Françoise Collin, *Maurice Blanchot et la Question de l'écriture* (Paris: Gallimard, 1971); Philippe Boyer, *L'écarté(e)* (Paris: Seghers et Laffont, n.d.).

6. Roger Laporte and Bernard Noël, *Deux lectures de Maurice Blanchot* (Montpellier: Fata Morgana, n.d.).

7. Pierre Madaule, *Une tache sérieuse* (Paris: Gallimard, n.d.)

8. [A deep melancholy, a world-weariness felt by a generation of young Romanticists in nineteenth-century France.—Trans.]

9. [See "The Poet's Vision," note 6 above.—Trans.]

10. [Pages 5 and 31 of the English translation, *The Madness of the Day/La folie du jour.*—Trans.]

11. [Leon Chestov (1866–1938), emigrated from Russia to France. He found the elements of a philosophy of tragedy in the works of Nietzsche and Dostoevsky. Reason transforms the real into the necessary, thus destroying freedom, which subsists as nostalgia.—Trans.]

12. [*The Madness of the Day,* 12.—Trans.]

13. [Ibid., 12.—Trans.]

14. [Ibid., 11–12, with a minor alteration.—Trans.]

15. [Ibid., 11, slightly altered.—Trans.]

16. [Ibid., 12.—Trans.]

17. [An allusion to Pascal's phrase: "Le silence éternel de ces espaces infinis m'effraie." [The eternal silence of those infinite spaces frightens me.] *Pensées,* ed. Victor Giroud (Paris: Les Editions G. Crès et Cie, 1928), pensée no. 206, p. 89.—Trans.]

18. [*The Madness of the Day,* 9, translation modified.—Trans.]

19. [The French text of *Sur Maurice Blanchot* reads "Pourquoi frauduleux cet arrachement?" (Why [is] this tearing away fraudulent?)

But it is clear that the logic requires that "fraudulent" modify sleep, not the tearing away from sleep. I justify my modification on the basis of the earlier version of this text, published in February of 1975 in the *Cahiers trimestriels du Collectif Change*, vol. 22: 14–25. Although the later version, which contains a few changes and additions by Levinas, is generally superior, it seems plausible that the addition of some explicative material by Levinas brought about the error. In the following sentence, I reproduce the material added to the later version in italics. "Mais on est toujours rattrapé, toujours brutalement arraché au sommeil frauduleux, *à ce qui n'est pas position, à ce qui n'est pas thèse, à ce qui emporte comme libido.* Pourquoi frauduleux cet arrachement?" My translation assumes that the inserted material separated the "Pourquoi frauduleux?" from its referent, "sommeil," and that by an oversight it was instead linked to "arraché."—Trans.]

20. [Levinas refutes this doctrine of Bergson's in "God and Philosophy," which was also published in 1975. See *The Levinas Reader*, ed. Seán Hand (Oxford: Basil Blackwell, 1989), 188, n. 17. See also *Proper Names*, Foreword, note 2 above.—Trans.]

Index

Abraham, 12, 74, 77
absolute, 44
Agnon, 7–16
ahavat Israel, 8
Albertine, 102–104
alterity, 22, 25, 26, 32, 44, 103
altruism, 73, 169; altruistic, 166
Aminadab, 141, 158
anthropology, 24
anti-Semitic, 123
Aristotle, 112, 128
Auschwitz, 159

Bachelard, 96
Banquo (in *Macbeth*), 100
Baudelaire, 53, 96, 151
Beaufret, Jean, 78, 91
Being and Time, 71
Bender, Hans, 40, 43
Benjamin, Walter, 42, 43
Bergson, Henri, 3, 19–21, 26–27, 50, 60,
    99, 100, 110, 114
beyond (noun), 9, 11, 84, 93; beyond
    being, 16, 47, 51, 53, 54, 93; beyond
    the Good, 61, 86
Blanchot, Maurice, 52, 59, 86, 91,
    127–170
Bonald, Viscount Louis de, 89
Boyer, Philippe, 157
breathlessness of spirit, 153

Brunschvicg, Léon, 83
Buber, Martin, 6, 17–35, 42

Célan, Paul, 40–46, 169
Char, René, 127
Chestov, Leon, 42, 164
cogito, 4, 62, 145
Collin, Françoise, 150–152, 154, 157
Conatus, 84, 166
consciousness, 18, 33, 34, 48, 49, 80, 82,
    83, 86, 91, 109, 121, 137, 162, 166;
    self-consciousness, 165, 166
cynics, 116

deconstruction, 58, 6
"deep past," 8, 56, 137
Delhomme, Jeanne, 47–54
Delmas, André, 150, 152, 154
Derrida, Jacques, 55–62
Descartes, René, 19, 61
diacony, 74
dialogue, 25, 26, 33, 34, 41, 42, 102,
    142, 144, 163
diaspora, 11
Diogenes, 117
Dostoyevsky, 100, 154
doxography, 111
durée, 3, 19, 24, 114

egology, 18

Einfühlung, 27
Eleatics, 24, 104
election, 73, 122
epistemology, 34
epochē, 48
errancy, of being, 133, 134; call to, 135
Estaunié, Édouard, 103
ethics, 16, 32, 61, 76, 101; ethical, the, 72, 73, 76–93; ethical stage, 67, 77; ethical elements of the I-Thou, 29; ethical meaning, 31–32
Ethics (Spinoza), 71, 83, 84
existence, 86, 104, 112, 116, 146, 159, 162, 169
existentialism, 48; existentialist, 72, 159

face, 4, 31, 64, 65, 73, 95–97, 137
Feuerbach, 23
Fink, Eugen, 53, 107
fourfoldness, 138
Freud, 82, 99
friendship, 33, 36–39, 104, 112
fundamentum inconcussum, 4
Fürsorge, 33, 37

Gabirol, Ibn, 14, 130
Genesis, 84, 97
Gogol, 10

Ha Esh Veha Etzim, 12
Hegel, 5, 45, 66, 70, 72, 76, 83, 86, 113, 114, 116, 128, 129, 142, 150, 153; neo-Hegelianism, 71, 76, 128
Heidegger, 3, 19–21, 23, 25, 32–33, 40, 71, 76, 78, 91, 113, 114, 127–129, 134, 136–138, 150, 152, 153, 159; see also *Being and Time*
Heraclitus, 27, 115
Hersch, Jeanne, 76
Hitler, 45, 108, 119; Hitlerism, 107
Höderlin, 42, 46, 127, 129
Husserl, 3–4, 19, 21, 30, 53, 56, 58, 83, 106, 107; Archives, 108

Isaac (biblical), 12; sacrificice of, 74

Jabès, Edmond, *passim*, 63–65

Jankélévitch, Vladimir, 29, 92, 130
Johanan, Rabbi, 38
justice, 119, 120; 137, 138, 146, 147

Kafka, 42, 127, 131
Kant, 60, 83, 153; Kantianism, 55, 110, 111, 150; "idea in the Kantian sense," 58
Kierkegaard, 28, 33, 66–79, 92
Kierkegaard vivant, 75
Koyré, 107

Lachelier, 102
Lacroix, Jean, 80–89
Landgrebe, Ludwig, 107
Laporte, Roger, 90–93, 157
L'attente L'oubli, 59, 141–143, 145, 152, 161
Lermontov, Mikhail Yuryevich, 148
Le Très Haut, 158

Madaule, Pierre, 157
Madness of the Day, 158, 159
Maistre, Count Joseph de, 89
Malebranche, 42, 43
Mallarmé, 46, 127, 129, 131
Malraux, André, *Man's Fate*, 51, 135
Marcel, Gabriel, 5, 6, 75
Marxism, 71, 82; Marx, 112, 116
meeting, 22–24, 29, 31, 35, 37
Melitsah, 9
Meridian, the, 41, 46
Merleau-Ponty, Maurice, 107
Minerva (owl of), 128
Miteinandersein, 19
Monde du silence, 96
money, 38, 113
Müller, Max, 107

National Socialism, 76, 106
natura naturata, 84
neighbor, 6, 16, 40, 41, 44, 93; love of one's, 85
Nietzsche, 24, 72, 82, 84; see also Zarathustra
Noël, Bernard, 157
nomadism, 137

non-indifference, 4, 6

ontic illusion, 57

ontology, 5–6, 9, 10, 14, 18, 23–24, 46, 47, 49, 53, 61, 71, 86–88, 162, 167; ontological, 103, 153

Parmenides, 105
Parmenides, 17, 19, 25, 53
Pascal, Blaise, 42, 71
Paulhan, Jean, 154
peace, 98, 104
Phaedrus, 51, 57
Picard, Max, 90–98
Plato, 4, 17, 19, 23, 25, 32, 51, 57, 113, 116; his "parricide," 61; cave allegory, 34; see also *Parmenides*, *Republic*, *Sophist*
Poe, Edgar Allan, 132
presence, 55, 57, 58, 60, 61, 80, 84, 90, 104, 152, 160, 162
Proust, 99–105
Psalm 139, 65
psychism, 50

Remembrance of Things Past, 100, 147
representation, 30
Republic, The, 113
resurrection, 12, 15, 16
revelation, 40, 78, 129, 130
Ribot, 100, 102
Ricoeur, Paul, 82, 107
Rilke, Rainer Maria, 42, 127, 129

Said, the, 5–6, 8, 11, 40, 59–61, 81, 143, 148, 156, 158
Sartre, Jean-Paul, 100, 102
Saying, the, 5, 6, 8, 11, 12, 40, 59, 61, 81, 93, 163
Scheler, 53
Scriptures, 8, 12, 14
Sein des Seienden, 23
Shakespeare, 100
skepticism, 57–59
sobering up, 163, 165

Song of Songs, 158
Sophist, The, 19
Speech and Phenomena, 56, 57
Spinozism, 85, 86, 89; see *Ethics*, *Theologico-Political Treatise*
Strette, 45
Subject, 17–20, 23, 40, 66, 74, 77, 90, 113, 128, 161; transcendental, 108; subjective, 101; subjectivity, 61, 64, 67, 70, 76, 92, 114, 123, 128, 145; anti-subjectivism, 50; subjectivism, 70–71
substitution, 61, 88
Surrealism, 141

Talmud, 65
theodicies, 16
Theologico-Political Treatise, 84
theology, 92
Thomas the Obscure, 152, 161
Thou, 6, 20, 22, 25, 26, 28, 31, 32, 35, 42, 132
Torah, 13, 15, 16
totalitarianism, 88
totality, 24, 34, 73, 86–87, 113, 147, 148, 154
totalization, 87
trace, 95, 149, 153
Trakel, 42
True, the, 79
truth, 17–20, 26–28, 32, 34, 41, 57, 59, 66, 70, 72, 77, 78, 87, 92, 100, 117, 121, 128, 130, 134–137, 149, 163

Une voix de fin silence, 90

Valéry, Paul, 140
Van Breda, Herman Leo, 106–109

Wahl, Jean, 5, 110–118
Weil, Eric, 107
Weil, Simone, 92
Worlds-behind-the-world, 81, 129, 155

Zarathustra, 49
Zwischen, 23, 24, 30, 33, 34

—

M E R I D I A N

Crossing Aesthetics

Emmanuel Levinas, *Proper Names*

Jean-Luc Nancy, *The Muses*

Alexander García Düttmann, *At Odds with AIDS: Thinking and Talking About a Virus*

Massimo Cacciari, *Posthumous People: Vienna at the Turning Point*

Ernst Bloch, *Literary Essays*

David E. Wellbery, *The Specular Moment: Goethe's Early Lyric and the Beginnings of Romanticism*

Edmond Jabès, *The Little Book of Unsuspected Subversion*

Hans-Jost Frey, *Studies in Poetic Discourse: Mallarmé, Baudelaire, Rimbaud, Hölderlin*

Pierre Bourdieu, *The Rules of Art: Genesis and Structure of the Literary Field*

Nicolas Abraham, *Rhythms: On the Work, Translation, and Psychoanalysis*

Jacques Derrida, *On the Name*

David Wills, *Prosthesis*

Maurice Blanchot, *The Work of Fire*

Jacques Derrida, *Points. . . : Interviews, 1974–1994*

J. Hillis Miller, *Topographies*

Philippe Lacoue-Labarthe, *Musica Ficta (Figures of Wagner)*

Jacques Derrida, *Aporias*

Emmanuel Lévinas, *Outside the Subject*

Jean-François Lyotard, *Lessons on the Analytic of the Sublime*

Peter Fenves, *"Chatter": Language and History in Kierkegaard*

Jean-Luc Nancy, *The Experience of Freedom*

Jean-Joseph Goux, *Oedipus, Philosopher*

Haun Saussy, *The Problem of a Chinese Aesthetic*

Jean-Luc Nancy, *The Birth to Presence*